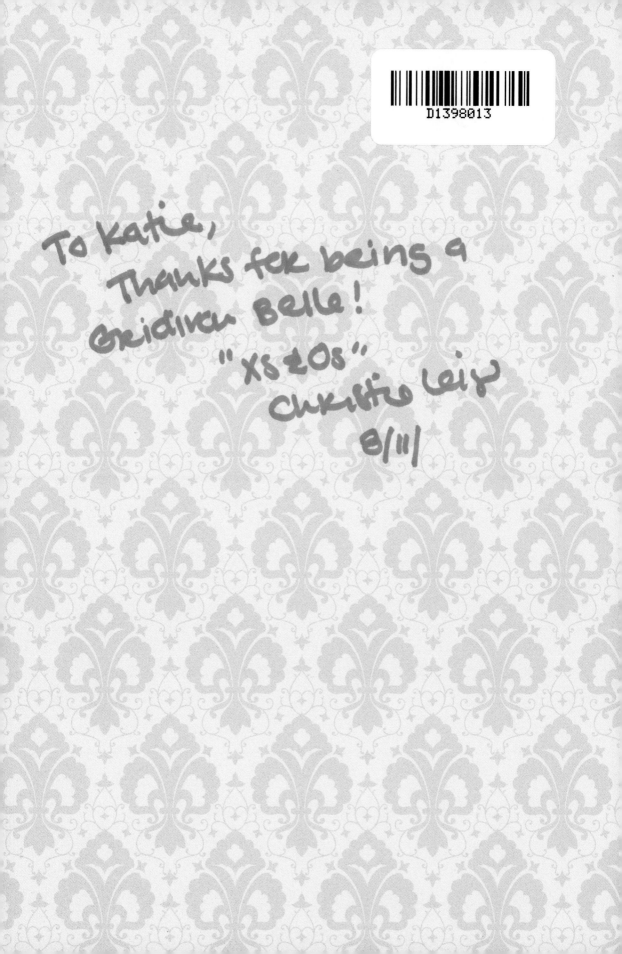

To Katie,
Thanks for being a
Gridiron Belle!
"XS ZOS"
Christie Leigh
8/11/

GRIDIRON *Belles*

A Guide to Saturdays in Dixie

CHRISTIE LEIGH MUELLER

GRIDIRON
Belles

A Guide to Saturdays in Dixie

CHRISTIE LEIGH MUELLER

Special thanks to all of the beautiful Belles who allowed me
to photograph them and contributed pictures to be used.

ISBN: 978-1-935497-43-1

Printed in Canada

Designed by Scott Stortz

Illustrated by Rachel Titsworth

Published by
Christie Leigh Mueller
P.O. Box 7753
Louisville, KY 40257
www.gridironbelles.com

For my grandmothers:

Jean "Momo" Porco and Rosie "Nan" Mueller

For showing me just how important the game of football is and for teaching me that dreams are achieved by a series of first downs, not "Hail Marys."

Table of Contents

Introduction

Dear Gridiron Belle,

Pour some sweet tea, find a front-porch swing, and take a seat. We are going to sit a spell and become old friends while I tell you a little about myself and how my uncompromising obsession with the gridiron began.

Born and raised in Kentucky, some of my earliest memories consist of family gatherings scheduled around kickoffs. My grand*mothers* instilled in me the joys of fandom and my deep appreciation of pigskin when I was just knee-high to a grasshopper. I learned how to throw an accurate spiral before I wore my first smear of lipstick or strand of pearls. Time and again, football has remained a source of happiness. It's one of my favorite topics of conversation, even during the off-season.

During my college years, even though I went to a liberal arts school in Tennessee, football became a means for acquiring many a boyfriend. Simply put, I began to realize that women can enjoy football as much as men do. The marriage of football and belledom began to materialize, giving birth to the term that makes my heart sing: Gridiron Belle. It is my hope that you catch the infectious spirit of the season—football season that is!

During the past few years, I've had an indescribable experience visiting all twelve SEC stadiums on game day, sharing one of the South's greatest rituals with old and new friends. Rival fans have welcomed me with open arms, despite my deep allegiance to a little team by the name of Auburn.

I have witnessed things that are considered acceptable only in our beloved quadrant of the country: *real* alligator heads as tailgate centerpieces, small children taunting rival fans, and families coming together once a year for the Ole Miss - Mississippi State game in lieu of a Thanksgiving meal. If I've learned nothing else on my stadium tour, it's that ambivalent hearts do not exist in Dixie. No one pulls for Vandy *and* Tennessee. No one cheers for Alabama "when they aren't playing Auburn." I didn't meet anybody who has both Arkansas and LSU, or Florida and South Carolina shirts in their closets. SEC enthusiasts are devoted to *their* team. It doesn't matter *why* they are a fan; it just matters that they *are* a fan.

My goal is to provide Belles of Dixie, "Belles in training" (those about to experience their first semester or Saturday at an SEC school), and Yankee transplants (bless their hearts) with insight into game day traditions, the Xs and Os of the game, and, of course, the unwavering pride that comes with cheering for any of the beloved twelve teams south of the Mason Dixon.

If you're already a Gridiron Belle (a Belle who embraces football season in its entirety), you are fully aware that Saturdays in Dixie are the greatest twelve days of the year. You swoon over crisp fall weather, game day traditions, tailgate delicacies, and the scent of bourbon wafting over stadiums. You know about fanatical supporters; you've memorized the Top 25 Poll, even though you know it will go out the window after the first snap of the season. And don't forget the sense of pride that does not falter! I am honored to be in your company.

If you are like my sister, who would rather be trying on bathing suits in the middle of winter than sitting in a stadium for four hours, this book is also for you. Southern football isn't just about the game; it's about the party, friends, and creating tailgating memories that'll last a lifetime.

Perhaps you don't consider yourself a Gridiron Belle just yet. But if you are interested in becoming one, here's what you have to accept:

- You are required to have fun at least twelve Saturdays per year, while most often wearing pearls.

- You must pass on to your female relations the Southern gridiron traditions of hospitality and civility while supporting your team.

- You are expected to accept without judgment the fan who eats, breathes, and sleeps football.

The rest of the country calls it football season, but down South, we call it heaven. And when we die, we are going to an SEC stadium where every day is game day. As Hank Jr. used to sing, "If Heaven ain't a lot like Dixie, I don't want to go."

From the fifty-yard line of the South, welcome to the gridiron!

Xs and Os,

Christie Leigh

Becoming a Gridiron Belle

The details that we Belles would have learned by taking snaps or running routes during our childhood days in Little League have left many of us perplexed by the particulars of the game of football. Thankfully, being a Gridiron Belle does not require one to understand every play called during a Saturday match up, enjoy every play, or even watch every game. Being a Gridiron Belle simply means that you understand the passion surrounding Southern football and how it governs many a Gent and Belle's universe. Be it from the actual Xs and Os or wins and losses or the festivities that allow Southerners to be some of the most socially graced fans of the game, being a Gridiron Belle means you dive in head first to take part in the tradition.

I also thought you'd appreciate knowing what still confuses other Belles and what the gents think you should know!

What Confuses You About Football?

"How each play is different from the last. They all look the same to me!"
Amanda Richmond, Mississippi State

"I have a hard time picking up holds and reading defenses. I also don't understand weddings in the fall, or BAMA fans in general." **Kelly Haywood, Auburn**

"I don't understand why Southern schools have noon games in September. It's far too hot. It's just cruel." **Sarah Hart, Florida**

How to Navigate the World of SEC Football

You know how they say the South has a language all its own? So does SEC football. Since the number one purpose of this book is to help you understand and enjoy the gridiron, below is a key to familiarize you with the most common phrases and terms you'll hear in Dixie and throughout this Belle-bible.

SCHOOLS:

Florida – FL or UF, Gators, The Swamp

Georgia – UGA, DAWGS, Athens, Between the Hedges

Kentucky – UK, Cats, Lexington

South Carolina – USC, Cocks

Tennessee – UT, Vols, Vol Navy

Vanderbilt – Vandy, 'Dores

Alabama – BAMA, The Tide, T-Town

Arkansas – Ark, Razorbacks, Hogs, The Ozarks

Auburn – Tigers, Plainsmen, The Plains

Louisiana State University – LSU, Tigers, The Bayou, Death Valley

Mississippi – Ole Miss, Rebels, Hotty Toddy, The Grove

Mississippi State – STATE, MS State or Bulldogs

MASCOTS:

Alabama: Big Al is an elephant, yet Alabama is commonly referred to as The Tide. Throughout the book, you will see me reference The Tide instead of an elephant. Just go with it.

Arkansas: Razorbacks are technically hogs. Arkansas fans are famous for "calling the hogs." I'll use Razorbacks and Hogs interchangeably, so try to keep up!

Auburn: Auburn does not have two mascots; they have a mascot (Aubie the Tiger) and a battle cry (War Eagle!). Fans and students of the Auburn Tigers are also referred to as Plainsmen (and women).

Florida: When you read about the Gators, you will be reading about the University of Florida. You may also come across "The Swamp," "Chompers," or "Albert and Alberta" (team mascots). All refer to Florida.

Georgia: "Uga IV," Uga is pronounced like the warm boots, Uggs, but with a long "a" ("Ugg-A"). Add a Roman numeral after Uga and you've got the name of the Georgia mascot. The Roman numeral describes the number of Ugas that have predeceased the current bulldog. When written in capital letters, 'UGA' means the university; when written with only the letter U capitalized, (Uga) it refers to the mascot. "DAWGS" refers to the university fandom. Both UGA and Uga are encompassed by the incorrectly spelled DAWGS.

Kentucky: The Kentucky Wildcats are commonly referred to as CATS. That's fairly simple, right?

LSU: A Bengal tiger is LSU's mascot. Death Valley is the stadium nickname. While Death Valley propaganda could all distract and intimidate opponents, Mike the Tiger does it best.

Mississippi: Ole Miss used to have "Colonel Reb" as its mascot. Many people in the community thought Colonel Reb tied Ole Miss to the days of slavery; thus, Colonel Reb was retired and replaced by Rebel Black Bear. Ole Miss fans are still encouraged to cheer for the "Rebels," but the on-field mascot is Rebel Black Bear. To Ole Miss fans, a "Hot Toddy" is a drink; "hotty toddy" is a battle cry. And you thought your family politics were complicated.

Mississippi State: The official mascot of STATE is a bulldog, yet you find more cowbells at a tailgate in Starksville than you do live bulldogs. When you read of bulldogs in this book, I'm probably referring to UGA; when you read of cowbells, be certain that I am referring to Mississippi State.

South Carolina: The South Carolina mascot is Cocky the Gamecock. You will hear South Carolina fans yell, "Go Cocks." I have tried my darndest to avoid writing "Cocks" when "South Carolina" will suffice.

Tennessee: Volunteering is honorable, but it's a hard mascot to symbolize at a game. Thus, the Tennessee Vols have a second mascot, a hound dog named "Smokey." I always refer to Tennessee as the Vols or UT.

Vanderbilt: The Commodores are the mascot of Vanderbilt; yet most of the time I refer to them as "Vandy" or the "'Dores." Their tailgating and spirit rarely gain the spotlight, but be assured tailgating in Nashville is alive and well, especially when a big-name SEC team rolls into town.

POSITIONS:

Defensive Back – DB or D-Back

Defensive Tackle – DT

Line of Scrimmage – LOS

Offensive Line(man) – O-Line

Quarter Back – QB

Running Back – RB

Tight End – TE

Touchdown — TD

Wide Receiver – WR

Could You Ever Date a Belle Who Didn't Enjoy or Understand Football?

Gents Say

"Yes, but she has to understand that for September, October, and November, I am somewhat preoccupied." **Russ Allen, Vanderbilt**

"Sometimes it's funny when someone I'm dating doesn't know what things like safeties are. But for the most part, as long as a girl is willing to tolerate the sudden rash of profanity during game time and understands the passion, she'd be good to go." **Zach Stovall, Arkansas**

"It happened to me once in college. We met in the first quarter, and we broke-up just before halftime. So I guess my answer is *NO*." **Michael Hart, Florida**

"No, I married a UGA grad well-versed in the nuances of college football." **Olin Arnold, Georgia**

"I couldn't date a girl who didn't enjoy football. For something I look forward to year around, the last thing I want is a miserable complainer sitting next to me." **Clay Harris, LSU**

"I could date her, but she shouldn't say much during the game." **Alabama Fan**

"If she just didn't know the game, that'd be okay, as long as she was interested and open-minded. If she actively disliked the game, well, I can't even really imagine such a situation."
Warren Kroges, Tennessee

"It would be tough, but I think I would enjoy showing her all that the game had to offer."
Alex Brey, Georgia

"Chances are, no. If I took a girl to a game, and she did not try to pretend to have a good time, then it would be over. Complain about the heat? Goodbye, you're in the South, darlin'. Don't understand the rules? Chances are, while I am trying to explain what "holding" is, I will be missing a game-changing play." **Calhoun Hipp, III South Carolina**

"Of course, as long as she doesn't tell me I cannot watch football on Saturday."
Joe Whitt, III, Alabama

"I don't think I could date a girl that had absolutely no interest in football. I'm not saying she has to be an expert or even a big fan, but I would at least like her to have some interest in the game and a team to cheer for." **Jack Porco, Kentucky**

"One who doesn't understand the game isn't a big deal to me, I can work with that. But one who doesn't even enjoy the game or the atmosphere, that's a tough one. Her enjoying going to football games is a HUGE plus." **Pat Manning, Auburn**

"Only if she lets me watch football all day with my friends." **Florida Fan**

"Yes. But I wouldn't be able to take her to the games if that's what you're asking."
Rob Williams, Kentucky

"There is nothing sexier than a girl who wants me to explain football to her. If she smiles at me while I talk about the best way to beat a cover-two defense, I'm sold. A girl who just doesn't understand, though, has great potential to be one of those who will listen and enjoy while I talk football. That's where it's is." **Charles Preuter, Bama**

"Yes, only if she is willing to let me teach her the game or the basics. If she refused to attend games or hated college football, then we probably weren't meant to be together in the first place."
Ralls Rinch, Auburn

"Never." **Tommy Kute, Tennessee**

"I don't want her cheering against me, I know that. And I would never date an Auburn fan. It just wouldn't be worth it." **Butch Case, Alabama**

Ladies, This is a Football

Despite the heated rivalries, football in the South is as much about spending time with friends and family and cheering for your alma mater as it is about understanding every formation and play. If you understand the game, it's an added bonus. If you understand the importance of tailgating and the camaraderie inspired by the color you are wearing, you've already got this most important part figured out.

If you've never watched a football game, don't fret—the rest of this book will describe plays, vocabulary words, and the method of scoring to give you as much or as little information about football as you want to know. For now, take in the big picture!

- Each team has eleven players on the field.

- Each play is broken down into offense, defense, and special teams.

- "Xs and Os" refers to a team's strategy, not how you sign your love letters. The X represents the defense, the O represents the offense.

- The offense and defense line up on the Line of Scrimmage (LOS) at the beginning of each play.

- The goal of the offense is to run, pass, or kick the ball down the field and ultimately over the end line.

- The goal of the defense is to tackle the man with the ball and prevent the offense from running, passing, or kicking the ball over the end line.

- It is your responsibility to cheer with reckless abandon for the men wearing your team's colors.

THE YELLOW LINE. This yellow line is found only on TV. The producers will use technology to produce a yellow line across your view of the field (your TV) to indicate where the first down spot is. There will not be a yellow line on the field if you are watching from a stadium.

THE BLUE LINE. The blue line, like the yellow line, is also found only on TV. The producers will use technology to produce a blue (or another color of their choice) line across your view of the field (your TV) to indicate the line of scrimmage (where each play starts). There will not be a blue line on the field if you are watching from a stadium.

THE RED BOX. The red box is known as the "Red Zone;" most people just call it "the Red." The producers will use technology to produce a red box encompassing the area of the field from the 20-yard line to the end zone. There will not be a red box on the field.

REPLAYS. Watch and listen closely to replays. Replays are slowed down to show the details of the play, and the commentators explain what's going on in a way that a 6-year-old (raised in the South) could understand. They will even sometimes use a magic pen to circle the penalty, highlight the call, or show the movement of the ball. Ask questions during a commercial if you still need clarification.

IF YOU'RE WATCHING FROM THE STANDS:

CHAIN GANG. Keep an eye on the sideline officials who carry the first-down chains. Two individuals will hold the ends of the chains(attached to two big orange poles). One will stand where the ball is initially placed, and the other official will move ten yards up field. This spot represents the line where the offense is entitled to a first down. Once your team crosses that invisible first-down line, cheer! If you're still not sure what's happening, wait for the stadium to erupt, and then join in!

Jumbotron. Jumbotrons are your best friend. If you can't tell from the stands where the first-down spot is, if a player was out of bounds, or if he actually scored a touchdown, watch the replay on the Jumbotron. You'll see the play up close, and you'll have a chance to boo if the officials missed an obvious call!

Extra Point:

Oh, and please, do not be caught on your cell phone while the camera crew is panning the crowd. If you're in a stadium and your seats are good enough to get you on the Jumbotron, it is common courtesy to be interested in the game! Despite my sister's petitions, magazines are not allowed in the stadium. If you're bored, read the media guide (aka the program).

What is Most Important for a Belle to Know About Football?

Gents Say:

"The game is never, never, decided in the first half, especially in the SEC. All big games eventually come down to who can make plays in the fourth quarter. Don't waste all of your energy in the first quarter because you'll definitely need it, come fourth quarter time!" **Pat Manning, Auburn**

"Which team she is pulling for." **Clay Harris, LSU**

"Cheer when fellow fans cheer." **Mississippi State Fan**

"Your purse must be large enough for two pints of whisky, and you must bring the tampons/pads to cover the bottles as we go in to the stadium. I got the tickets; you carry the booze."
Tommy Kute, Tennessee

"Really, it is not all about the football. I think it is important for belles to know that football is a lot about going to new places, enjoying fun people, the food, drinks etc. **Alex Brey, Georgia**

"Football is important to me. If she understands that, then she will be cool."
Brandon Hudspeth, Ole Miss

"Pay attention to who has the ball.
Don't cheer when an opponent on the field is hurt.
Know the basic positions: quarterback, running back, wide receiver, etc.
Don't leave until the game is over. (There might be some disagreement on this one, but it is a stickler for me.)
Be quiet during the National Anthem (this should go without saying, but there is always somebody)."
Joe Whitt, III, Alabama

"Knowing positions help a lot, but it's more important to support your team and friends/spouse after a loss." **James Stozier, Auburn**

"Don't complain about things you know nothing about, specifically officiating and coaching. If you are knowledgeable, then by all means, go ahead. Also, I'm sorry to say, you're not priority #1 on gameday. Non-negotiable. Please understand that." **Rob Williams, Kentucky**

"Understand why football is a religion in the South. Understand why it makes or breaks a Saturday. Understand why the fans put so much heart into every game, that they deserve to refer to the team as 'we.' Understand the game and the way of life of Southern football."
Calhoun Hipp, III, South Carolina

"For players, football in its purest form is not about touchdowns and tackles. It is about loyalty to the name on the front of the jersey. It is love for the boys out there, who you know will never let you down. And it is about playing your heart out for the people watching, the ones who care about you: parents, fans, and maybe even a special girl to call yours." **Charles Preuter, Alabama**

"Know the traditions and history of your team. Understanding why there is a Hounds Tooth Hat at BAMA, or why you show up eight hours before game time to celebrate. SEC football is as much about the social interaction as it is about the game. You see old friends and relive what you did ten, twenty, thirty years ago, when you were in school. Your team is your sense of pride; therefore, you support them with all that you have." **Russ Allen, Vanderbilt**

"Cheer for your team when they do well, and boo the opposing team every chance you get. Make as much noise as you can when the other team is on offense. It's a scientific fact that defense wins championships." **Olin Arnold, Georgia**

"I don't think there's any concept or rule that's more important than the others. Just have a basic familiarity with the rules of the game so she can follow along and enjoy the game."
Warren Kroges, Tennessee

"Follow the ball, the action follows the pigskin." **Mark Robinson, Georgia**

How to Score on the Field

Touchdown	6 points	Safety	2 points
Field goal	3 points	Extra Point	1 point

A **touchdown** is scored when the ball is carried or passed over the end line (the line separating the field from the end zone).

If the ball is being passed over the end line, the player receiving the ball must have at least one foot in bounds and have control of the ball. The receiver cannot be fumbling the ball in his hands; he must show that he has control of the ball.

If the ball is being carried (or run) over the end line, the ball needs only to break the plane of the end line. Imagine a piece of glass going from the ground to the sky at the end line. If the ball touches the glass and breaks it, it's a touchdown. The ball does not need to go completely through the "glass;" it just needs to break it. Of course, everyone feels better when the whole ball crosses the plane!

A **field goal** is scored when the ball is kicked through the goal posts, also known as uprights. A successful field goal will award your team three points. Most teams will kick a field goal when they are too far away from the end line to run or pass for a touchdown. The kicking team, or special teams unit, will kick the ball. The distance for field goals varies. If the kick is considered too great a distance, the offense will punt the ball to the defense's return team. It is up to the offense (the kicking team) to assess where they are on the field and decide when it's time to kick.

A **safety** is scored when the defense prevents the offense from getting out of its own end zone. This might happen if the offense takes too long to get rid of the ball and the QB is sacked (tackled while still carrying the ball), or if a RB is tackled in the end zone. A safety can also be awarded if the offense commits a penalty in its own end zone.

An **extra point** is a field goal kicked immediately after a touchdown, earning the kicking team one point. The distance for field goals does not change; the ball is kicked from the 10-yard line, which is actually a 20-yard field goal because of the 10 additional yards from the end zone to the goal posts.

Saturdays v. Sundays

Thanks to TV rights and scheduling, you can catch a battle in the trenches on almost any night of the week during football season! However, the greatest days in the fall are still Saturdays when the vast majority of college football is played. A close second, if you follow professional football, is Sunday, when the vast majority of professional football games are played.

Because many of our SEC gridiron heroes continue to play football at the professional level, it's important to be aware of the differences between when our boys play on Saturdays (NCAA) and on Sundays (NFL), or at least to know that there *are* some differences!

Days of Play:

NCAA: Saturday, with some games on Thursday and Friday

NFL: Sunday, with big games on Monday

Leagues of Play:

NCAA: National Collegiate Athletic Association

NFL: National Football League

Completed Pass:

NCAA: Only one foot must be in bounds for the pass to be completed.

NFL: Both feet must be in bounds for the pass to be completed.

"He's Down!":

NCAA: If a player falls, or his body (other than his feet and hands) touches the ground, he is considered down and the play must stop.

NFL: If a player falls and his knee or body touches the ground and he is not touched by an opponent, he may get up and continue running.

Overtime:

NCAA: Overtime does not have a time limit. Each team has four downs to score, starting from the 25-yard line. Play continues until one team does not score or does not score enough points.

NFL: Overtime period is 15 minutes and is "sudden death." In other words, the first team to score wins the game.

Show me the Money:

NCAA: Schools make millions

NFL: Players make millions

Pass Interference:

NCAA: The maximum amount of yardage a team can gain is 15 yards. If the penalty occurs 50 yards down the field, the ball is placed 15 yards from the line of scrimmage. If the penalty is called less than 15 yards from the LOS, then the ball is placed at the spot of the foul.

NFL: The penalty is a "spot foul" meaning the ball will be placed at the spot where the foul takes place. A penalty 50 yards down the field could potentially be a 50-yard penalty.

Extra Point:

PASS INTERFERENCE

NCAA: If a defensive player tips the ball, contact between players is allowed.
All is fair in love and football.

NFL: Automatic first down and the ball is placed at location of foul.
It would be like getting Jimmy Choo shoes on sale and the second pair free.

What Will You Teach Your Daughters About Football?

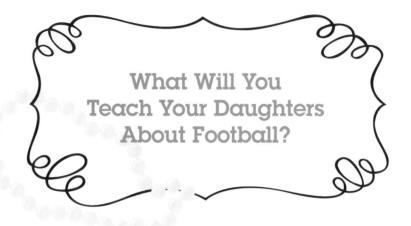

Gents Say:

"How to throw a spiral." **Warren Kroges, Tennessee**

"Football is a religion in the South with the only break during the weekend being for church on Sunday." **Olin Arnold, Georgia**

"I'll try to explain the traditions of the SEC and Ole Miss, and the importance of a good tailgate." **Brandon Hudspeth, Ole Miss**

"Date an offensive lineman. They'll keep you centered, protect you, and hold you from time to time." **Michael Hart, Florida**

"I'll bring them along for the ride. Explain things, but never be overwhelming or over-assuming. Those that tailgate together stay together..." **Alex Bray, Georgia**

"If I have a daughter, I will teach her to understand the game and to love and respect it. I will also teach her

to never marry a boy who doesn't like college football.
I will teach her no matter how many times her team
may break her heart, they are still her team, and she
has to stick with them throughout."
Calhoun Hipp, III South Carolina

"I don't think football is only an interest a father and
son can share; it is extremely important for a young belle to
grow up knowing about football." **Jack Porco, Kentucky**

"Don't date football players." **Ryan Horton, Georgia**

"Never let a man put football first. No daughter of mine
will ever let a man make her feel like football is more
important than she is."**Charles Preuter, Alabama**

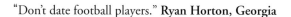

Meet the Team

It's not necessary for you to know every position on the field, but it is important for you to be familiar with the overarching theme of each position. Sometimes it's just nice to be able to translate the meaning of "I used to play tight end in high school" from the new Gent you are dating. Maybe he has a tight end, but in this context, it means much more!

Football basics come down to three things: offense, defense and special teams.

When your team is on offense (the "O"), its goal is to score, hopefully more often than the other team.

When your team is on defense (the "X"), its goal is to prevent the other team from scoring, again, hopefully more often than the other team.

Extra Point

The yellow Xs and Os and route lines you often see drawn on TV are not on the actual field. Players do not have the advantage of following the lines. They are drawn by commentators and appear to fans, thanks to special effects.

The special teams unit is on the field when your team is kicking (or punting to the other team), returning the kick, (catching the ball and trying to run as far as possible toward the end line) or blocking the other team from kicking.

The team with the most points at the end of the game wins: the rivalry, the bragging rights, and the SEC pride…at least for that particular season.

When your team gets the ball, they score points; when they don't have the ball, they block the other team from scoring points. Voila! Your team wins. You might think of a football game like Sorority Rush. The basics are similar: Go to the houses, meet people, impress people and voila! You're a pledge.

Alas, we all know there is much more to eternal sisterhood, and this is true for Xs and Os.

Below are the breakdowns of the offensive and defensive players. Just as it takes more than the president to run a sorority house, it takes more than one star quarterback to win a championship.

OFFENSE

Offensive Linemen

The "O-Line," also known as the group that battles "in the trenches," consists of the offensive players on the line of scrimmage. Their goal is to protect the ball-carrier while simultaneously creating gaps on the field where the ball-carrier can safely run through the opponent. The offensive linemen are the *big* guys.

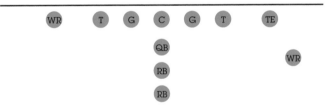

Offensive line (O-line) positions from left to right: Tackle, Guard, Center, Guard, Tackle.

Center

The play starts with the center snapping the ball (passing the ball through his legs) to a teammate. Once he snaps the ball, he begins to hold off the oncoming opponents.

Extra Point:

The Center is not an eligible receiver. Meaning, the Center cannot catch the ball even if he is the only open teammate of the quarterback.

Guard

There are two guards on every line of scrimmage, one on each side of the center. The guards do what it sounds like: They *guard* the quarterback, or whoever has the ball, from the opponent.

> There must be seven players on the line of scrimmage and four in the backfield.

Tackle

There are two offensive tackles who line up on the outside of the guards. They try to block (or tackle) the opponent before he gets to the quarterback, or the player with the ball.

Tight End

Tight ends line up on the line of scrimmage next to one of the tackles, and they are supposed to have the dual abilities of blocking linemen and receiving passes. Tight end is a hybrid position between offensive lineman and wide receiver (see below).

Wide Receiver

A wide receiver lines up on, or near, the line of scrimmage. His primary responsibility is to catch passes. These players are generally fast and tall, so they can get down the field to catch passes and elude defenders.

"Spiking the ball"

(throwing the ball directly into the ground) is considered an incomplete pass. In a hurry-up mode (when the clock is running out), the quarterback will spike the ball to stop the clock. This strategy is helpful when a team is out of time-outs or when the clock is winding down, and the team needs a break to plan a last-second play.

Backfield

The backfield is the part of the field behind the line of scrimmage. Fullbacks and halfbacks are types of running backs, and they usually line up in the backfield.

Fullback/Running Back

The fullback either blocks for the halfback so he can run down the field, or the fullback blocks so that the quarterback can make an uninterrupted throw down the field. A fullback is generally bigger (or "fuller") than the halfback and is capable of running the ball, but he typically runs for shorter distances than the halfback.

Halfback/Running Back

The halfback lines up in the offensive backfield behind the fullback and the quarterback. The halfback primarily runs the ball during running plays, such as The Option (see "offensive plays" in the Vocabulary section). He can also be used as a wide receiver. Halfbacks are usually fast and powerful, capable of breaking through defenses or running around them.

Quarterback
(ALSO KNOWN AS THE QB)

The quarterback is usually the most well-known player on the team. He is responsible for a quick scan of the field, determining the appropriate play, and notifying his team which play to execute. The quarterback takes the snap (receives the ball from the center), and he can choose to hand the ball to the running back, pass the ball to an eligible receiver, or run the ball himself. Great quarterbacks are proficient at all three. Tim Tebow of Florida and Cam Newton of Auburn were exceptionally large and dynamic quarterbacks who were not afraid to run the ball themselves, but who were more than capable of throwing accurate passes.

> **"Taking a knee"** is a way for the offense to use time off of the clock, and minimizing the chances of turning over the ball. The quarterback will simply take the snap and then lower his knee to the ground. You see this most often toward the very end of games when a team is winning and just wants to end the game and go celebrate.

DEFENSE

Defensive Linemen

The defensive line consists of four linemen (two ends and two tackles) who line up directly across from the opposing O-line.

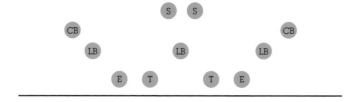

Defensive line from left to right: End, Tackle, Tackle, End.

End (Tight End)

A defensive end lines up at the *end* of the defensive line. The defensive end's main purpose is to contain the running backs to the inside on running plays, or to rush the quarterback on passing plays.

Tackle

Tackles are responsible for stopping the run up the middle and for engaging the offensive linemen so that the linebackers can move toward the ball without opposition.

Nose-Guard

This player is also known as the nose-*tackle*. Depending on the defensive scheme (line up), defenses will have what is called a nose-guard. This player lines up directly over the football (his nose is over the ball)— not necessary to know, but good vocab.

Linebacker

Linebackers are the second line of defense and line up behind the defensive line, in front of the secondary (defined below). Most teams have either three or four linebackers, depending on their chosen formation. Their goal is to stop the run, defend against passes, and sometimes, to rush the QB (Quarterback). Linebackers are usually faster than defensive linemen and are larger than their defensive teammates. They also aren't afraid to hit people with their broad shoulders.

Secondary

Secondary is the area of the field that is off the line of scrimmage (way in the back) where defensive backs (cornerbacks and safeties) are strategically placed to defend the run and pass.

Cornerback

A defensive back, who lines up off the line of scrimmage (LOS) and is usually responsible for covering wide receivers. Cornerbacks need to be fast to cover and catch up with receivers.

Safety

A safety is the last line of defense and is extremely fast and aggressive. He can serve as an eraser and clean up mistakes (i.e. missed tackles). Safeties are found deep in the defensive secondary (way in the back) and help the cornerbacks with pass coverage. They are supposed to tackle their opponent before he crosses the end zone with the ball.

"If you're mad at your kid, you can either raise him to be a nose-tackle or send him out to play on the freeway. It's about the same." – Bob Golic

SPECIAL TEAMS

Special teams units are made up of players with specific skills, who are not typically starters. They participate in all transition plays, including punts, field goals on fourth downs, and kick offs at the beginning of each half.

KICKING TEAMS

Gunner

The gunner is usually the fastest player in the unit. His main goal is to tackle the kicker or punt returner and contain him.

Holder

The holder receives the snap from the center and holds the ball for the kicker. The holder is sometimes the same person as the punter, because he is used to catching snaps. His primary purpose is to avoid fumbling the ball and to hold the ball in good kicking-position, with the ball's laces facing the goal post, for the place kicker. Just remember, "laces out!"

Long Snapper

The long snapper can also play the position of center but usually does not. The long snapper specializes in longer snaps (longer than a normal snap to a quarterback) for punts and field goals to improve probability for a successful punt or kick.

Extra Point:

A typical shotgun snap to the QB is 4-5 yards. A typical snap from the long snapper to the punter is about 14 yards.

Place Kicker

This player is usually referred to as the "kicker" and is responsible for kicking field goals through the goal posts, extra-points after a touchdown, and kickoffs at the beginning of the game, at a quarter, or after your team scores.

Punter

The punter stands behind the LOS and receives the ball from the long snapper. The punter is usually called onto the field on 4th downs to punt the ball deep into the opponent's territory.

RECEIVING TEAMS

Kick Returner

The kick returner's goal is to get as far down the field with the ball as possible. This player needs to be fast and is frequently a player who is used to catching the ball and running. Generally, the kick returner is a backup receiver or running back.

DEFENSIVE SPECIAL TEAMS

Punt Returner

Similar to the kick returner, the purpose of the punt returner is to catch the punt and run toward the end zone or to catch the ball and wave a fair catch (wave his arms in the air to signify that he is not going to attempt to run, thus avoiding being tackled by the other team).

Extra Point:

When the players are running on and off the field, they are doing so because they are either changing from offense to defense, defense to offense, or to make way for the special teams unit.

Put me in, Coach!

It sounds like the beginning of a bad joke. But really, how many coaches does it take to coach a football team? The punch line can fluctuate, but on average, each team has approximately 10-15 coaches who vary in role, responsibility and expertise.

While head coaches are often as hard to keep track of as a game of musical chairs, I strongly encourage all Gridiron Belles to know each of the head coaches in the SEC. You'll receive extra points from fellow fans for knowing a few offensive and defensive coordinators of your own team and your opponent's.

Extra Point

Gracefully demonstrating knowledge of top recruits who were brought to your team by your assistant coaches is really pouring it on, but it equates to going for a two-point conversion (going for two points after a touchdown) in overtime during a championship game. And that's major.

COACHING STRUCTURE

Head Coach

The head coach makes all of the major decisions, including when to punt, when to go for a touchdown on the 4th down, and when to kick a field goal. He is the most recognizable coach of the team. Consider the head coach the President and his coordinators and assistant coaches as his cabinet members. Each assistant coach is responsible for a specific realm of expertise and then reports back to the head coach to relay updates and final approval. As a rule of thumb, the bigger the school's football program, (read: the greater the championships and the booster intake) the more coaches that pace the sidelines and sit in the booth.

The Coordinators

All coordinators are considered assistant coaches, but they each have different responsibilities. Offensive and defensive coordinators call the offensive and defensive plays, respectively, and may be responsible for one additional position. For example, the offensive coordinator may also serve as the quarterback coach.

Don't forget about the assistant coordinators and some position coaches who sit in an elevated coaches' booth in the stands. They take advantage of this bird's eye view when advising the head coach to challenge a penalty or which play to call next. These assistants are the people who are whispering sweet nothings into the field coaches' headsets.

Position Coaches

Generally, each position on the field is assigned an individual coach. When the positions he coaches are not on the field, the position coach is instructing those players on the sidelines.

Recruitment

The majority of college recruiting is conducted by assistant coaches. The head coach makes calls and appearances for major recruiting instances. Many assistant coaches and coordinators become ideal prospects when head coaching positions become available.

Graduate assistants:

Graduate assistants are also valuable assets on the coaching staff. Graduate assistants will fill in wherever there is a shortage of coaches, and they do most of the preliminary film study for upcoming opponents.

Men in Stripes

Everyone loves to hate referees. Officials earn a pretty penny for making controversial calls, taking the brunt of countless bad jokes, and serving as scapegoats for poor skills, bad coaching, and lazy players. Fans sometimes harass and taunt referees more than they do the other team. That being said, a Belle becoming incredulous over what she thinks is a major injustice, but is actually a good call, is perhaps the most common game day faux pas.

While you don't need to know every difference between a holding penalty and an illegal block penalty, you do need to know when to pipe up and when to pipe down. (And if you *do* want to know the difference between holding and an illegal block, those are in the "Pretty Yellow Flags" chapter.)

Here are the basics on the men (and on very rare occasion the women) in the striped uniforms:

- The Officiating Crew is composed of seven referees.

- These "refs" are technically called "officials," because only one actual referee is present: the guy with the "R" on his back and the white hat.

- This team of officials is responsible for making sure that no one gets hurt and that everyone plays nice in the sand box.

Officials and their full job descriptions are located in the Vocabulary section. For the time being, learn from what your fellow Belles asked:

How do the officials know when the player has reached a first down?

The officials are supported by the "Chain Gang." The Chain Gang consists of off-field officials who are responsible for marking and measuring yardage progress by the offense. You can see the two-person gang standing on the sideline with two triangular orange poles (for lack of a better term).

When a first down is too close to call for the officials on the field, the Chain Gang will come out on the field and mark where the ball is spotted.

Extra Point

The yellow line on TV does not show up on the field; please refrain from asking where the yellow line is. Asking the location of this television-generated line is a MAJOR faux-pas! Few things can blow your Gridiron Belle status more quickly. An Ole Miss fan once told me that comments like this earn his wife "chip duty."

What does it mean for a play to be "under review?"

Each coach is allotted two reviews per half. If the referee makes a call with which the coach disagrees (a touchdown, pass interference, or a player stepping out of bounds, etc.), the coach can throw his red review flag, and the head referee will review the play.

During the review, the head referee watches video footage of the play from several different angles. In order to change the call (the ruling) on the field, the review must provide sufficient evidence to overturn the call. Otherwise, "the ruling on the field stands."

If the call is changed, the coach does not lose a time out. If the ruling on the field does not change, the coach loses a time out. If you are sitting in the stands and it's not a time out of any sort, but there is no activity on the field, chances are a play is under review.

Why is the official in the way?

There are seven officials on the field, each with his own purview. The officials are positioned on the field according to the fouls and regulations they are watching for; thus, they have to be in the thick of the action.

Extra Point

If an official is blocking your view, it's really not worth complaining about. Simply turn around to watch the play on the Jumbotron if it really puts a tangle in your hair.

Who is that guy with a red hat standing on the field?

That's the TV official. He stands on the field while the network goes to a commercial during timeouts, injuries, and any other instance when the network might take a break to show its love for advertisers.

While waiting for "Red Hat" can be frustrating, go ahead and keep your seat to rest your feet. Play cannot resume until he heads to the sideline.

What's in those yellow things?

Those yellow things are called penalty flags, and they are usually filled with sand, corn or BBs to allow for accuracy when signaling a penalty. Officials throw a flag (the pretty yellow things) when they see a penalty occur on the field. Some officials will even carry more than one flag in their pocket at a time in case more than one penalty occurs.

Then why did the official throw that white beanbag?

The white, or sometimes blue, beanbag is a spotter. This can be used to spot where a player went out of bounds, where a player went down, where a fumble occurred, or where a punt was caught.

Why do officials get together before they announce the call?

Officials gather to discuss a call for the same reasons you might get together with friends to discuss the latest gossip—more perspectives provide more accuracy. If one official makes the call, but another official saw the play differently, they will discuss which had the better angle and how the rules apply.

How can a team decline a penalty? Is that a nice way to say "No thanks?"

In a way, yes, the offense is saying "no thanks" to the less advantageous penalty.

Keep this rule in mind: the *offended* team always has the choice of *penalty or play.* This means that a team can chose to take the yardage from a penalty, or the yardage they gained from the play, depending on which gives the greater advantage.

For example, a call such as, "defensive holding down field on the defense (holding a receiver)" is a 10-yard penalty. But if the offended team had a 15-yard gain (or more than a 10-yard gain) on the play, they will decline the penalty because they earned more yards on the play than the penalty would give them.

Think of it like shopping: if one store's offering 20% off that orange and blue sundress you've been eyeing, and the store next door is offering it at a regular price that's even lower, you're better off saying "no thanks" to the sale price.

> "I'm not allowed to comment on lousy officiating."
>
> – Jim Finks, when asked after a loss what he thought of the refs.

Pretty Yellow Flags

Even officials, ex-players, and obsessed Gents sometimes have a hard time *accurately* "calling" a game and knowing the appropriate yardage associated with each penalty. So I don't want to bore you here with a list of penalties that are rarely used. Instead, I have included the most common calls with some helpful explanations that you certainly don't need to memorize.

When a lively debate erupts, there is no need for Belles to interrupt to ask questions, especially if it's a tied game late in the 4th quarter. Instead, head to wherever you've stashed this book and do some quick research! Or just listen to the debate and laugh to yourself about how worked up everyone gets. Remember, Gridiron Belles don't have to make the calls or argue the penalties to be true fans; being a Gridiron Belle is about enjoying the game and the company you keep.

Extra Point

Just to be clear, each penalty call is accompanied by a pretty yellow flag thrown by the officials. When you see a flag flying through the air, feel free to yell "flag!" Something has gone wrong and the current play is in question.

Clipping

Blocking below the waist from behind. This tactic is considered dirty and is likely to cause an injury. Belles might think of clipping with the same disdain that you'd feel for someone who'd expose her best friend's secrets during a fight. As Florida fan Jack Massey says, "It's just not right."
Penalty: 15 yards

Delay of Game

Failing to start the play (snapping the ball) before the play clock runs out. Belles who run late for a game can relate to this predicament; it's the most common Belle-penalty committed on game day. Putting time constraints on pre-game primping may work in the Big 10, but this is the SEC. Go ahead and throw the flag, a Belle must get ready! **Penalty: 5 yards**

Encroachment

Crossing the line of scrimmage and causing a set offensive player to move, or making contact with the opponent, before the ball has been snapped. This is the same as intentionally flirting with someone else's gent with hopes of luring him to make a move. Find your own Gent. There are plenty down here. **Penalty: 5 yards**

Facemask

This penalty is exactly what it sounds like: when someone grabs his opponent's face mask. This is the easiest one for an observer to call before the officials throw a flag. After all of that primping, you wouldn't want anyone touching your face either! **Penalty: 15 yards plus automatic first-down.**

False Start

When an offensive player moves or flinches before the ball is snapped. This player is too excited, too soon. Think of an overly-excited Belle hinting at a left-hand diamond on the third date. It's just too soon. **Penalty: 5 yards.**

Forward Lateral

An offensive player passes the ball forward after crossing the LOS. All forward passes must originate behind the line of scrimmage. **Penalty: 10 yards**

Holding

An offensive player, usually a lineman, holds onto an opponent, rather than blocking from the front shoulder pads. Holding prohibits the defensive player from moving freely or from moving toward the ball. Belles can relate. Ever have Gent refuse to let you dump his poor little heart? **Penalty: 10 yards, replay the down.**

Extra Point

Defensive holding is the opposite of offensive holding. Usually this penalty is called on defensive players who are attempting to prevent a receiver from catching the ball or tackling a non-ball carrying player during a play. This results in an automatic first down being awarded.

Illegal Block in the Back

Whenever a player blocks a non-ball-carrying player by way other than front shoulder pads. A player cannot block or tackle another player without fair warning. Belles, don't start dating someone new until you give your current Gent plenty of fair warning; it's just not ladylike. **Penalty: 10 yards.**

Illegal Contact

A defensive player makes contact with a receiver before the ball is in the air. Belles liken this call to a Gent who makes a move on a friend's object of desire before he has time to seal the deal. **Penalty: 5 yards and automatic first down.**

Illegal Man Down Field

An illegal receiver catches the ball. Belles, this is the same as your gent doing more than "just hanging out" with your best friend. **Penalty: 5 yards.**

Illegal Procedure or Motion

Bad formation. When less than seven offensive players are present on the LOS or a back is moving forward at the time of the snap. This is also called if a player takes more than the allotted two steps after waiving a fair catch. Belles, this is similar to a freshman Belle or Gent coming to a tailgate in shorts and a t-shirt. There are some things you just don't do. **Penalty: 10 yards.**

Illegal use of Hands or Feet

The name says it all. You'll rarely see this called in a game, but it is often called late at night in bars across SEC towns. **Penalty: 10 yards**

Illegal Substitution

When a team has twelve or more men in a huddle for more than three to five seconds. Also called when twelve or more players are in the formation, or a twelfth player is still on the field (even if leaving the field) when the ball is snapped. This is just like a typical Saturday night cab ride home. Your entire pledge class just isn't going to fit! **Penalty: 5 yards**

Intentional Grounding

When a quarterback throws an obviously uncatchable pass to rid himself of the ball and avoid being tackled. The quarterback needs to at least try to salvage the play. This is the same as Belles prematurely throwing out their empty mini bottles of bourbon in the stadium entrance line to avoid getting caught by stadium police. **Penalty: Spot of foul, loss of down.**

Offsides

If a defensive player is on the wrong side of the LOS while the ball is snapped, he is offsides. This penalty applies even if he does not touch another player before the ball is snapped. Looking like you're being unladylike is just as bad as being unladylike. **Penalty: 5 yards.**

Pass Interference

When a player interferes with an opponent's opportunity to catch the ball while the ball is in the air. If the pass is deemed uncatchable, no penalty is called. **Penalty: 15 yards or spot of the foul.**

Extra Point

If a defensive player tips the passed ball, contact is allowed.
All is fair in love and football.

Personal Foul

Playing dirty. (Well, being obvious about it, at least.) **Penalty: 15 yards**

Roughing the Kicker

A defender intentionally making contact with the kicker, usually during a punt, extra point or field-goal attempt. For Belles, this penalty is similar to intentionally contacting your ex against your better judgment. **Penalty: 15 yards, automatic first-down.**

Running into the Kicker

A defender unintentionally runs into the kicker while his leg is still in the air. This penalty would be like coincidentally running into your ex at your old stomping grounds. Sometimes a Belle just can't help it, but the damage is the same. **Penalty: 5 yards**

Spearing

A player tackles another player leading with his helmet. This penalty is highly discouraged, so much so that it may eventually become a reason to be ejected from the game. Helmet-to-helmet contact is terrible manners. When the other team goes for a helmet-to-helmet tackle, you should absolutely flip your pancakes in the stands! There is no need to hurt our boys intentionally.
Penalty: 15 yards

Tripping

Using a leg to "trip tackle" the opponent. An effective, yet unladylike way for a Belle to trip someone she dislikes. **Penalty: 10 yards.**

Unnecessary Roughness

Making contact with another player after the play is completed. When you see a player from the other team hit your players after the play, yell out "Where's the flag?!" Usually, the flag is on its way, but it shows that you are paying attention, *and* you know it's a penalty. **Penalty: 15 yards**

Unsportsmanlike Conduct

This penalty is called if a player spikes the ball; gets in the face of another player; continues to tackle, jump, kick, or hit after the play is dead; or participates in flagrant or choreographed celebrating after a touchdown (this could also be called Excessive Celebration.) In the case of a touchdown, the touchdown stands, but fifteen yards is given to the opposing team on the next kickoff.

Belles should refrain from commenting on this penalty if it's called for excessive celebration after a touchdown. After all, who isn't going to celebrate a touchdown against an SEC team? In the immortal words of my sister, "Don't they all do a little dance?" **Penalty: 15 yards**

The BCS v. The Playoffs– Which Wins a Belle's Heart?

The Bowl Championship Series, commonly referred to as the BCS, is the equivalent of a long-term boyfriend who you just won't marry. Sure, the BCS has its perks. It showers you with entertainment, value, and often a surprise that is just what you wanted. But alas, the savvy Belle knows that, like the going-on-seven-years boyfriend who's left you dissatisfied or disgruntled way more than once, the BCS could be better.

Perhaps against our better judgment we accept (even embrace) the BCS for yet another season because, even though we know it's not perfect, it's comfortable.

But what about throwing caution to the wind and checking out Mr. Playoff? Is that an attempt to marry for money that provides better game day outfits and box seats? Surely that's what more games and longer TV contracts would provide, right?

It's enough to make a Belle wish there was a hybrid: a gentleman with the body of a quarterback *and* box seats, enough know-how to fix us a bourbon, and the common sense to avoid important questions on Saturdays during games. Do we believe that we'll be happy and comfortable enough again one day to desert what we already have, which (let's face it) isn't all that bad?

Just so you know what you're saying "I do" to, here are some pros, cons, and facts about the BCS and the other likely eligible suitor competing for your heart during Bowl Season.

The current boyfriend, affectionately called BCS:

How it works:

You (read: your team) date the BCS throughout the regular season. For those three months, you are judged. Harshly. Coaches, analysts, and even computers not only quantify your worth each week, but also rank you according to an obscure numerical value. As the season comes to an end, no matter what injuries you've suffered or what promises you've made, those judges vote on your future.

- A pool of selected voters decide which bowl game, if any, you will play in, essentially determining the revenues your school and your conference will receive for your success (read: your dowry). Think arranged marriages that benefit bank accounts but fall short of your fairy tale dream.

- The team with the highest score is ranked #1. (BCS rankings are published each Sunday, starting midway through the season.)

- At the end of the season, the #1 and #2 BCS ranked teams play in the BCS National Championship

- The remaining BCS bowls (and your boyfriend) often pick teams that may not be the best at football but are sexy and will bring them the most money. The truth hurts...

BUT LET'S NOT KICK BCS TO THE CURB JUST YET.

- Remember: A few losses here and there may not be too detrimental if you play in, say, the SEC, have a history of winning seasons, or perform consistently. This actually affects the strength of the schedule, improving your BCS ranking. Either way, dating a Belle like you would improve anyone's BCS ranking.

"Oh, hey Mr. Playoff"

The hotter, more exciting, still a money-maker but less comforting, fairest boyfriend answers to "Mr. Playoff."

Mr. Playoff advocates equality, or so he says, for all of his friends who have worked hard throughout the season. He is a noble contributor to society who believes that the best man (team) should be crowned the victor of the Belle (read: the title). He does not depend on armchair quarterbacks or computers that can't even run a route to decide the championship. He prefers objectivity and survival of the fittest, even if it means his team isn't winning.

Rest assured, this free-market system does not mean that your newest Gent likes basketball (gasp!) more than football. This means his clear-minded and brilliant way of thinking may just be the comfort you are yearning for after finally breaking up with BCS. If nothing else, it's a welcomed change.

Before you rush into Mr. Playoff's free lovin' arms, you need to know:

- Playoffs, the system that all other major competitions use in baseball, basketball and softball, would cause our boys to play additional games during December, increasing chances for injury.

- Playoffs would be great for the top eight conferences, making it difficult for a non-automatic qualifying conference to ever have a BCS bowl game presence (read: the smaller programs would have a harder time advancing).

- There would still have to be some sort of controversial tie breaker for all teams that tie with the same record at the end of regular season.

Here is a sample of what Mr. Playoff believes in:

🏈 Eight conference champions play in a post-season "tournament."

🏈 The last two teams standing play each other. The winner is crowned National Champion.

🏈 The winner has proven it can beat every team in the country, no computer needed. (You can cancel your online dating profile.)

Before the indecision sets your heart into a flurry, remember that BCS and Mr. Playoff are not your only options. There's still hope that one day we'll find a happy medium: a man that can love us unconditionally and fairly, a man that does not come with baggage or controversy. Let us exercise the virtue of patience here.

Trust me, I know it takes a while to get over the computers and comfort of BCS, but give yourself time. You may never forget the BCS, but you'll love again. After all, you deserve a champion.

Why We Give the Heisman

"The Heisman" has many meanings in the world of football. For the football arena, it refers to a prestigious award that receives as much TV coverage as a presidential election. For the Belle domain, the famous "stiff arm" is something we are good at giving to unappealing suitors of the unwashed nature. I strongly encourage you becoming proficient in both!

It's important for Belles to know the origins of this widely-coveted trophy. It's named after Mr. John William Heisman, the player and coach responsible for instituting significant changes in the game, such as the practice of a center snapping the ball (versus rolling the ball), and making the forward pass legal. Below you'll find a few more basics that will help you carry on conversation and earn some extra points from your Gent with facts and trivia about the famous "stiff arm."

Heisman Essentials:

- The Heisman is an annual award presented to the best football player of the season.

- Coaches, football reporters, commentators, and former Heisman Trophy winners each receive one vote for their favorite candidate.

- The award was formerly known as the Downtown Athletic Club Trophy, which is where Mr. Heisman served as Athletic Director. The Downtown Athletic Club is located in New York City.

- The solid bronze Heisman trophy weighs 45 pounds.

- The Heisman is not exclusively an offensive award; however, recipients tend to be offensive players, due to their ability to acquire easily comparable statistics (touchdowns, rushing yards, and pass completion percentages).

Extra Point

One exception is Charlie Woodson (1997) of Michigan, who was a cornerback. Tennessee fans are still hot that their beloved quarterback, Peyton Manning, was passed over in favor of Woodson.

- In the modern day of media coverage, most Heisman winners are accompanied by winning teams.

- Winners of the Heisman Trophy have formed one of the most elite fraternities in the country and are often esteemed for decades by their team.

- "Heisman Hopeful" is a term used by overzealous commentators and fans to describe the potential of a player during the upcoming season. Potential is usually based on previous season's stats, improvements during off-season training, and coaches' comments. These predictions are often more hype than fact.

- Talk of Heisman Hopefuls begins in the off-season, long before the first kickoff flies. You could apply the term to your favorite player when you're chatting. Once the season begins and your player's statistics aren't as impressive as you'd hoped, it would be a good idea to develop a sense of humor or thick skin, because you might get teased.

- For the superstitious, "the curse of the Heisman" supposedly precludes any winner from winning the national championship in the same year he is crowned Heisman.

- Only five people have proved that curse a hoax: Danny Wuerffel (Florida, 1996); Matt Leinart (USC, 2004); Tim Tebow (Florida, 2007, first ever sophomore to win); Mark Ingram (Alabama, 2009); Cam Newton (Auburn, 2010).

—   Steve Spurrier won the Heisman in 1966 as quarterback for Florida and later won the national championship as coach of Florida in 1996.

—   John Heisman was elected to the College Football Hall of Fame in 1954.

SEC Heisman Trophy Winners

YEAR	NAME	SCHOOL	POSITION	CLASS
1942	Frank Sinkwich	Georgia	RB	Sr.
1959	Billy Cannon	LSU	RB	Sr.
1966	Steve Spurrier	Florida	QB	Sr.
1971	Pat Sullivan	Auburn	QB	Sr.
1980	George Rogers	South Carolina	RB	Sr.
1982	Herschel Walker	Georgia	RB	Jr.
1985	Bo Jackson	Auburn	RB	Sr.
1996	Danny Wuerffel	Florida	QB	Sr.
2007	Tim Tebow	Florida	QB	Soph.
2009	Mark Ingram	Alabama	RB	Soph.
2010	Cameron Newton	Auburn	QB	Jr.

Cramming for Conversation

How on earth is a Belle supposed to prepare for football season and learn everything about her team's off-season, win-loss-record, coaches, players, schedule, injuries and weekly challenges?

Let's face it, we are all busy living our lives Sunday through Friday and would call a week sitting behind a computer or in front of a TV researching statistics nothing more than dull. We also know that Belles become nothing more than dull at a tailgate if they cannot keep up with the conversation about a beloved team. What's a girl to do? It's simple: channel your college days when you were balancing mid-terms with frat parties and cram before the big test on game day.

Think of this list of resources as the class notes you access before heading to your tailgate or watch party. These can be quick references or indepth studies. You just need a few key stats (if the staring QB is injured, if they beat this team last year, if these coaches don't get along, if they are debuting new uniforms this week, etc.) to get a conversation going. If all you can contribute to a football conversation is one or two things, that's great. Other people should be able to broaden their topics of discussion as well!

RESOURCES:

SEC Media Days

Consider SEC Media Days Christmas in July. At at press conference in July, all SEC coaches give a report on their team's spring training, summer practices, and how their offenses and defenses are shaping up for the fall. Reporters ask countless questions about starting positions, tough schedules, previous scandals and ominous predictions. This is when you get a good sense of coaches' personalities and his confidence in your team.

Media Days are the true kickoff to the season, so listen closely! The information you hear on these days will be the basis of many fall stories to come. Your blood will be dancing in your veins, fight songs will fill your brain and your fall schedule will all of a sudden revolve around nothing but the gridiron.

ESPN's College Gameday

The easiest and most entertaining way to learn the basics about your team is by watching College Gameday on ESPN on Saturday mornings. Hosts Lee Corso, Kirk Herbstriet and Chris Fowler spend an entire week studying up on all of the facts of college football and deliver you highlights on an HD silver platter.

If you pay attention to when they cover your game, you'll be set to understand and contribute to most of the chatter surrounding it. If you feel like going for some extra credit, listen to the hosts of College Gameday cover all of that weekend's games and how each outcome affects your team's standing; you'll be able to comprehend *all* of the chatter about college football that day!

College Gameday broadcasts live from one rival game site each week to the backdrop of crazily clad, diehard fans and will usually feature a special, usually heartwarming story, about a player from each school.

Extra Point

I've mastered straightening my hair and putting my face on while watching College Gameday. If applying mascara and curling your hair with one eye is too much, keep the bathroom door open and turn up the volume—this information is as essential as your ticket!

ESPN.com articles

Three to five minutes on ESPN's website and you're sure to see some good college football highlights, stories, and conversation about next week's games. I doubt you'll be off in five minutes once you find the tab that covers your team, but that's the point!

SportsCenter and the bottom line

If your Gent simply cannot go to sleep without watching SportsCenter, join him! How do you think Gents always know the latest in the football world? They watch SportsCenter, which brilliantly breaks up the day's big athletic news into bite-sized pieces that are easy to digest, even for Belles! Pay close attention when they start to cover the gridiron and listen to the blitz-like update. You should also keep an eye on the bottom line (that black and red line that scrolls across the bottom of the screen). It's loaded with snippets of breaking news as well as scores updated in real time.

Social Media Updates

If you have any Facebook/Twitter friends that are SEC fans, sign on and check out their posts. Fans can't seem to refrain from posting stories, comments, or updates about their team. Use this to your advantage to be in the know.

Sports Illustrated Covers

Glance one shelf to the left of *Cosmo*, *Glamour* and *Women's Health* to see what's on the cover of *Sports Illustrated* (commonly referred to as *SI*). If you see that it's a football player, you don't even have to read the article, just read the tag line under the picture. This way you can at least ask, "I saw Marcus Lattimore on the cover of *SI*, but didn't get to read it. What did it say?" Be prepared—with a question like that, and you're likely to get a detailed response and an excited Gent who thinks you're interested. You may even learn something!

Talk Radio

There is nothing more passionately biased than talk radio! If you're driving to your team's town, turn on AM talk radio to find out what the fans are saying about this week's game and the storm you are about to drive into. You'll hear more than you ever wanted to know about how your team is going to handle the opponent and what the coach should or shouldn't do with his players. While you'll inevitably learn some new perspectives, take in this pre-game-studying-festivity with a big smile. It's just passionate, salt-of-the-earth people talking about their team.

Say What?

Don't think you have anything to say at a tailgate? Of course you do! Simply asking a fan, "How are your DAWGS this year?" or "Is this your first time to Starkville?" is conversation gold. People *love* to talk about their team's glory and embarrassment and SEC experiences. Just get them going and chime in with what you learned on College Gameday and have observed thus far at the tailgate.

Speed Dial

It's prudent to have at least one well-versed Gent and one stellar Gridiron Belle on your speed dial for quick questions. These supporters will help you clarify a play, answer a team roster question and celebrate a win. Try not to overuse them, but honestly, no one really gets upset if you're asking about football in the middle of their otherwise mundane workday, off weekend or if their team is losing!

You've studied up, you're ready to head out to the tailgate, but you still wouldn't mind a little help in case you freeze up on-the-spot, right? Scribbling notes on the palm of your hand wouldn't be very Belle-like(or match your outfit), so take a cue from this cheat sheet I gave my sister the week before her first trip to the Swamp and first SEC football experience. Just like the individual SEC team chapters in this book, this brief cheat sheet gave her a few facts for an otherwise apathetic attendee. Of course, no cheat sheet in the world can fully prepare anyone for an SEC town on Saturdays, but it's a start!

Abigail's Cheat Sheet: Welcome to The Swamp
(IT'S WHAT THEY CALL THEIR STADIUM)

Our Team For This Game: Florida

Mascot: Gators (we'll practice your "chomp" in the car)

Colors: Blue and orange

Wardrobe to Pack: Royal blue and light orange, preppy sundresses and flip flops, hair up, Jorts are also welcomed if you want to go casual.

Projected Temperature: H-O-T-T

Appointments: -Leave Jacksonville 10:00am, (I know, sorry—it's a 13hr football day, no beach this time!)
- Park at Alleigh's house off of University
- Lunch at The Swamp (Watch South Carolina game, talk to handsome Gents for "interviews", show you how to converse with male fans)
- Balls for a drink (Doing this for the story; it's quite fratty for early in the day, but worth the trip.)
- 3:30 meet Sarah and Michael at Bull Gator Lot for a Painkiller and Swamp- tailgate-tour.
- 6:30 pm Enter stadium
- 7:30 pm Kickoff

Win-loss-record: You couldn't care less, but both teams are doing well and could use a win. Fans will be intense, embrace it.

Florida Quarterback: Brantley (Lots of people at tailgates will be comparing him to last year's QB, Tim Tebow)

Florida Running Back: Demps (FYI, he also runs track for UF, so he's one fast sonofagun)

Coach: Urban Meyer (May be his last year, watch closely!)

Opponent: LSU Tigers (this is the team your friend Camille cheers for)

LSU Quarterback: Jefferson and Jarrett Lee combo (Don't worry about it…)

Coach: Les Miles (Tricky coach, will likely call a trick play at last minute, don't fall asleep!)

How to Score Tickets

Acquiring tickets to an SEC game can be as easy as riding a bike or as difficult as saying "no" to half-price pitchers the night before a test.

You'll need a little preparation and a lot of luck to land a good seat (or any seat at all) at the best games of the year. There is a reason SEC stadiums are full every fall weekend; season ticket-holders don't let good seats go to waste. So how do you find these widely-coveted gems?

Your options are, but not limited to, the following:

- Call the school ticket office to see what seats they have left. If you don't mind where you sit, or if you're heading to a less-than-nail-biting game, you should be able to score a few tickets directly from the school.

- Turn your inheritance over to the university and get on the waiting list for season tickets. Donating to the school has its perks, like getting a library or a wing named after you, but SEC fans will happily cough up the dough in exchange for a chance to get great seats, year after year. That's right, the face value may say $45, but I assure you that ticket will end up costing you much more! Start young, get on the list early. Surely by the time your kids graduate from said school, you'll have tickets together. Maybe.

- Make friendly with someone who has already given a left arm to the university and has season tickets. It helps if you're dating someone who pulls for the same team, but if you aren't, never pass on a chance to attend an SEC game. Love is love; eventually, Florida will play Auburn.

- Talk at tailgates. Let a few people at your tailgate know that you're still looking for a ticket to the game. More than likely, somebody has a pledge sister whose cousin's mama-in-law has an extra ticket from her husband's old college roommate. And just like that, you've got a one-way ticket through the heavenly turnstiles.

- Head to the stadium with a purse-full of cash and hold your fingers in the air. You'll find countless scalpers offering some good, (and some not-so-good) deals on seats. Be sure to look at the seating chart on the back of the tickets before you part with your cash.

The beauty of searching for tickets in the SEC is the sheer fact that everyone wants you to experience the game. People are as generous with their tickets as they are with their tailgates. If a season ticket-holder is not making the trip that weekend, he or she will gladly give you his/her tickets and parking pass if you ask early and are a dedicated fan. No one likes to give up seats for a fair-weather or mediocre fan.

One more thing—if a season ticket-holder is kind enough to give you tickets, (and if you'd like to get the same seats next year) be gracious. Take some pictures of yourself enjoying the game and send them to your ticket donor along with a sincere thank-you note. A bottle of nice bourbon for their next tailgate doesn't hurt your chances either!

> LSU fan, Mr. Carey Roussel, is the most generous season ticket holder I know! He's happy to share his seats as long as I ask early and promise to wear purple and Gold!

When Whistles and First Downs Bore You

Gridiron Belledome isn't always love at first kickoff. If the thought of cheering for your team or spending every waking moment of the fall discussing gridiron topics doesn't make you weak in the knees, don't fret. The great (or not so great) news is, football is still right for you!

If whistles and first downs bore you, try these tactics:

- Socialize: Plenty of people are fans of tailgating and football season purely for social reasons—as they should be! Don't worry about not loving the game; just love sharing a cocktail and snack with great people dressed in similar colors. And yes, it's completely fine to chat in the stadium at your seats as long as you are not interrupting others around you, particularly your date!

- Practice your baking: Meticulously decorated cookies, cupcakes and other desserts in team colors can take your thoughts away from penalties and touchdowns and allow you to get in touch with your inner pastry chef.

- Challenge yourself: Making a seven-course meal look gourmet in Tupperware is harder than beating a national championship team!

- Bring binoculars: These are ideal for people who want a good view of the players' and coaches' best sides—and who occasionally like to watch the game. Binoculars are also must-haves if you'd rather people watch and go on fashion patrol.

- Offer to stay with the tent during the game: You will not be alone; plenty of other fans prefer to tailgate through all four quarters and into the night. Save on a ticket by parking yourself at your tent. Chat the night (or day) away with a comfortable seat and enjoy delicious fanfare!

Count how many live mascots and pets you see: Laugh to yourself as you count how many pets are named after school legends. Then, realize how many of your friends have named their children after the same legends!

Be the designated photographer: Catch all of the special moments for those who are enjoying the tailgate and the game. Pictures make great thank-you gifts, and, when put together in an album, can make for a fabulous birthday treat for your favorite fan.

Avoiding "Dip Duty"

"Dip Duty" is a term coined by an Ole Miss Gent, Matt Word, who explained that there are certain things Belles should never say during a football game. If they do, they might be regulated to the more mundane tasks of refilling the dip, chips, drinks, and other game day snacks instead of sitting down and enjoying the game.

Generally, the terms "inning," "slam-dunk," and "homerun" are among the top offenders. However, during the first four minutes of the 2010 LSU v. Florida game in The Swamp, my wing-belle and lovely sister, Abigail, exhaled an enormous sigh of boredom and frustration. She followed this dramatic breath by uttering six unforgettable words, "I should have brought a magazine."

Such gaffs uttered by Belles are less than ideal when others around you are trying to embrace and enjoy the ambiance and elation that accompanies the gridiron communities across Dixie. Thus, I have compiled a quick list of how to avoid "Dip Duty" in case you've ever looked for glossy reading material other than the media guide during a game.

What Should Belles Not Say During a Game?

Gents Say

"Under no circumstances should you comment on how handsome you think the opposing team's players are. Don't drink too much, and definitely, try not to talk too much or ask too many questions of your man during or after a loss." **Olin Arnold, Georgia**

"My feet hurt" **Tommy Kute, Tennessee**

"Do not talk about things while a play is going on that does not have anything to do with the current play, unless it's an emergency. (And by emergency, I don't mean how your sister's boyfriend just broke up with her.)" **Joe Whitt, III, Alabama**

"It's important to know when silence is golden. Try to keep ditsy comments to a minimum." **Jack Porco, Kentucky**

"Do not pull out your cell phone. Even if your date does. If he's worth his salt, he's only making sure Tennessee is losing." **Rob Williams, Kentucky**

"Anything that causes her date to miss the big play. Having to explain things over and over, and then missing the big play, can be quite frustrating. Whining is not tolerated under any circumstances." **Mark Robinson, Georgia**

"Inning. There is no reason for a Belle to ever use the word "inning" during a football game." **Matt Word, Ole Miss**

"Don't turn around to talk to people if you're at the game. The game is *that* way. No one cares that you and the girl four rows behind you are wearing the same thing." **Zach Stovall, Arkansas**

"Don't pass out." **Alex Brey, Georgia**

"Anything that will start a fight which I have to participate in." **Kentucky Fan**

"Cuss. I'll probably laugh about it, but it's not very lady-like." **Alabama Fan**

"I once had a girl ask me what the big yellow poles in the middle of the field were for (referring to the goalposts). I just looked at her, said nothing, and walked away." **Calhoun Hipp, III South Carolina**

The Ps and Qs of Xs and Os

Modern-day etiquette has evolved to fit our times. Thankfully, modern-day Saturdays in the South revolve around the gridiron. Belles thrive on hospitality, etiquette, and hosting an unforgettable tailgate. Your proficiency in all three of these can be showcased without your ever learning how many yards an offsides penalty receives. (It's five, by the way.)

To make those who came before us proud, honor the traditions of the SEC and keep the SEC's reputation for gentility alive and well, follow these Ps and Qs of the Xs and Os.

At away games or when visiting a friend's stadium:

- Know your venue. Ole Miss is different in attire, tailgating and play from any other team in the SEC. If you are a guest from another team, ask your hostess ahead of time what her usual game day attire is and dress accordingly! Your team jersey with tennis shoes may be welcomed in Arkansas, but anything less than a beautiful summer dress in The Grove is an insult to your hostess and to the team on the field.

- Socialize and be helpful. As an out-of-towner, your ability to make an award-winning appetizer is limited, but offering an extra pair of hands is your biggest gift. Take out trash, refill drinks and dips, or simply ease the burden of cleaning up afterward by making great conversation. Be sure to share your favorite parts of your experience with your host!

- If you are a guest to someone else's stadium, and his/her team is not playing your team, dress in the colors of your host's team. On the other hand, if your host has been kind enough to invite you to his/her stadium because the host's team is playing your team, you are more than welcome (in fact, strongly encouraged) to dress head-to-toe in your team's colors, minus face paint.

- Be prepared to be taunted by home-team tailgaters. As a guest, keep your bragging to a minimum if your team wins!

At home games:

- If it's your Saturday to play host, consider your tailgate your "home." It's your responsibility to make your guests feel comfortable. Offer drinks, food, and introductions.

- Tidy up. Respect your team and school by cleaning up after your tailgate. Whether you win or lose, do not leave a disaster for the custodial staff to attend to. Your diligence says that you care enough about tradition to come back next week, and you are doing your part to make sure the environment remains in good condition.

At any game:

- Lose with class. Opposing fans are going to be more hospitable to you if you handle your team's loss gracefully. You are more likely to be invited to their tailgate for an adult beverage to talk football if you congratulate opposing fans on a good game. Everyone will have a better time!

- Offer to bring some item to help the hostess or just show up with an always-necessary bag of ice and bottle of bourbon. In the South, we call this a "hostess gift," and a true Belle never arrives without one.

- Plastic sticks topped off with colored streamers are called shakers. When showing your enthusiasm via the omnipotent shaker, shake it with vigor! Just be sure to always shake it forward to avoid causing injury to those around you.

- Never go into a game hungry. Forget what Mammy from *Gone With the Wind* said about eating like a bird. Eat your heart out before kickoff (with your mouth closed, of course)!

- Witty banter is entertaining. What is not entertaining is watching an over-served fan make a sentence entirely out of four letter words. Make sure you and your date act in ways that reflect well upon you and your team.

Always send a thank-you note. Whether you were a guest at someone else's stadium, or someone was able to snag a coveted ticket to the championship game, be sure to make your hostess feel appreciated. But you already knew that...

Let your hair down and enjoy the opportunity to be with 100,000 of your closest friends in a setting that can be found in only twelve parts of the country. Relax and let the atmosphere do the work. Saturdays were made for celebrating being Southern!

Dressing for SEC Success

What do Belles wear to a game?

Belles Say

"Sunday best!" **Kailyn Aertker, Ole Miss**

"A cute outfit that incorporates orange and navy. It's very common to hear girls say, 'Oh, that would make a cute gameday outfit while shopping in February.'" **Peyton Gregory, Auburn**

"When it is warm, a dress, and when it is cold, leggings and a Courtney Upshaw jersey." **Jeanie Sleadd, Alabama**

"Maroon, white, or black dresses." **Amanda Richmond, Mississippi State**

"A cotton dress and flip flops. In the Florida heat we'll do anything to stay cool."
Sarah Hart, Florida

"Sundresses when it's early in the fall because it gets so hot. When it's colder, boots with skinny jeans and a festive sweater and accessories. A true UT fan always has an orange belt accessible."
Shelly Tasman, Tennessee

"I never get dressed up for games. I'm a real fan! Just a UK blue T-shirt for me. Or sweatshirt, or toboggan. I must be showing blue on game day, no matter what the weather!"
Lindsey Ranney, Kentucky

"I used to wear heels and a dress, now jeans and a T-shirt." **Morgan Roussel Volion, Auburn/LSU**

"Jeans, a black or white top, and cute orange accessories." **Julie Foster, Tennessee**

"I never, ever wear anything other than a dress." **Laura Neeley, Georgia**

"Something creatively spirited. But I always practice how my outfit is going to look with my cocktail!" **Palmer Brown, Ole Miss**

"Usually I wear a royal blue dress or white accented with orange and blue. Because it can be so hot, no pants! **Kelly Gooddard, Florida**

Your Wardrobe for Braving the SEC Elements

Whether we are cheering on our gridiron heroes in the September Southern sun or on frigid November nights, it's important to wear our game day-lovin' hearts on our sleeves. My research has concluded that the sexiest thing a Belle can wear to a football game, according to the Gents, is a sundress in her team's colors.

It is vital to our Belle personas to show our loyalties via our wardrobe. When you're shopping for fall clothing, be sure to purchase some go-to pieces in your team's colors. Don't forget accessories! With friends at every stadium, it is in our best interests to keep a few gold, red, orange, and purple staples pressed and ready for when the "I've got an extra ticket" call comes in.

The reality is, the South has weather hot enough to melt goal posts and cold enough to freeze bourbon. Here are the tried-and-tested tips for staying Belle-beautiful in the sweltering, sultry Southern heat and for staying cozy during the chill of bowl season.

Two-a-day H-O-T-T

Pray. It's Dixie, after all. Get on those Southern Baptist knees and pray that your seats are in the shade or that you know someone in a box. If your tailgate doesn't have a tent or a nearby tree, start batting those eyes and go find one that does. Nobody in their right mind will turn down a pretty little Belle who wants to join the party.

Hydrate. Drink lots of water and hope that you have a date who is sweet enough to constantly buy you bottled water and stadium cups full of ice!

Avoid dark clothes. Every team has light-colored uniforms, and as a fan, you should, too! Opt for the lighter shade of team spirit. For instance, if you're a South Carolina fan, go for white and accessorize with a garnet or black necklace, earrings, belt, or purse. Do *not* make the same mistake I made by wearing black *and* garnet with seats in the sun… you can see how well *that* turned out.

Sundresses and sunscreen. It's part of the Gent's Y-chromosome to swoon over Belles in sundresses. Wear a cotton sundress that can breathe against your skin and dry quickly in case your glisten gets aggressive or someone spills a beverage on you. Sunscreen protects your skin, allowing you to partake in the post-game victory celebrations instead of having to soak in aloe. Again, refer to the pictures below, where these rules were not followed.

A-Little-Dab'll-Do-Ya. Foundation is never flattering when it's melting. Because you will still be tan from the summer during the early season, there is no need to cover your face with loads of foundation to smooth your complexion. If you feel naked without makeup, use a tinted moisturizer with sunscreen and add mascara.

"Paint your lips to keep your man." According to Ms. Nina, an avid Ole Miss fan, we can all keep our men (and our classy looks) by frequently applying lip gloss. If you are a minimalist with makeup, more power to you. Just don't forget how a little gloss can single-handedly complete an outfit.

Wear a ponytail. Your hair may be beautiful when you go out in Athens on a Friday night, but on a September afternoon between the hedges, you are better off with a sleek (but not junior-miss-styled) up do. Keeping your hair off your neck not only keeps you cooler but prevents your hair from going flat and unsightly come halftime.

Seek and you shall find shade. Take several trips to the restroom to seek shade and wash your hands under cold water. Cold hands, wrists, and necks will keep your body temperature down to reduce the glistening.

Extra Point

Walking around also helps alleviate bleacher butt.

Flat shoes: Because you are invited to so many tailgates, you will have more ground to cover than the running back. Flat, sensible shoes are as important as a player's cleats. If heels are your thing, hide a pair of flats in your bag for later. Luckily for you, your options come in school colors and let your toes breathe!

Lighten up your drink. As a Kentucky girl, this is tough to say, but bourbon needs a break until late October. Bourbon is the unofficial-official drink of Saturdays in the SEC, but it's the official drink that will make you sweat like "Smokey" basking in the sun. Trust me; you won't be nearly as endearing as Smokey, that cute Coonhound.

If you're of the ripe old age of twenty-one or older, stick with clear alcohol. Be sure to alternate water drinks and liquor drinks. It won't completely prevent you from perspiring in 95-degree weather, but you will look much better than the novice who is trying to get some "color" in the sun while sipping hot bourbon in a black dress!

Glisten, don't sweat. Handkerchiefs may be found at antique stores, but they are by no means antiquated, especially on game day. When experiencing the inevitable glisten, avoid wiping your brow or upper lip. Blot. Most bookstores also sell battery-operated, handheld fans that are a clutch in the Southern heat. A Belle never sweats; she glistens!

It's Yankee Cold and We've Got a Game

Bring a good date. This goes without saying. The better your date, the warmer you'll be. Either you'll have his jacket, or he'll have his manly arms wrapped around you.

Be hospitable and share: Share your lucky stadium blanket, your body heat, and your bourbon with the people around you. After all, they cheer for the same team, which basically makes them kin.

Colorful layer-after-layer-after-layer! A chilly day game is bearable with the Southern sun. A night game during rival weekend requires additional heat-trapping team paraphernalia. Bring in that extra purple sweater or your red hat and gloves. Stash a couple of those feet and hand warmers in your pockets. Remember, the TV official on the field that is making us all wait for the next play is concerned with people watching the game from somewhere *inside*, not someone who is sitting in the elements, lacking all feeling in their extremities!

Bleacher seats. If you are watching the game from aluminum bleachers or concrete steps, bleacher seats are your best friend. Invest the $10 and get a bleacher seat that not only provides comfort but also serves as a two-inch barrier between the cold material and your darling backside. A date's lap also works, but that's only during timeouts and if he isn't interested in the game (in which case, I suggest a new date).

Hot-Toddys! Leave it to Ole Miss to get it right and know how to stay warm, win or lose. When the temperatures drop, bring back that bourbon. It will keep all teams warm during fourth-quarter drives. If hot-toddys aren't your thing, ask your date to bring hot chocolate or coffee.

Good makeup. Cold is the preferable weather for makeup, so take advantage. If it's too cold to abide by any team-oriented color schemes or outfit coordination, by all means, throw on your warmest jacket, hat (at least *try* to make your hat cute), turtle neck, etc. Add a small team logo face tattoo, and you're all set!

Ponchos are hot. It shouldn't be a surprise that most rainy games are also cold. It's always best to come prepared with a disposable poncho in your touchdown purse. Easily obtainable at any bookstore or from vendors at the tailgates, you cannot go wrong when you have one of these to cover your game day outfit, perfectly styled hair, and meticulously applied makeup.

Make friends with RV owners. You may prefer to tailgate on the lawn or gravel, and you may prefer the stadium to a plasma TV, but when you can't move your toes and you're up by two touchdowns, it might be best to just visit fellow fans in their well-heated mobile mansions.

Cheer! The more you jump up and down when your team scores, tackles, punts, or runs, the warmer you'll be. Let the excitement move you, literally! You'll be warm in no time, and will become known as a bigger fan than you imagined!

Extra Point:
GAME DAY WARDROBE ETIQUETTE

A Belle comments, but does not complain, about the weather. Everyone in the stadium is experiencing the same climate. We endure hell and high water for our teams. That's what makes SEC fans the best in the country. Fair-weather fans live over in the Pac 10.

"The reason women don't play football is because 11 of them would never wear the same outfit in public."

– Phyllis Diller

Wardrobe Essentials Checklist

✔ **Touchdown Purse:** A purse that adds style to your touchdown dance. A purse that has enough room for lipstick, camera, a beverage of choice if so desired, and plastic, but does not knock people over while you're getting to your seats in a crowded stadium. Reminder, if your purse does not fit comfortably on your shoulder during the game, it will be under your seat and susceptible to spills and peanut shells.

✔ **Sandals:** Find cute, flat sandals. Everyone will be happier.

✔ **One go-to game day outfit:** You can mix and match or add to this ensemble, but every Belle needs one team outfit that makes her feel like homecoming queen all over again. Minus the sequins.

✔ **Sunglasses:** Whether in pre-season or during bowl games, the sun shines over the SEC, and you need to look good in your sunglasses.

✔ **Handkerchief:** We are Belles. We do not sweat; we glisten. To keep your glistening in check, you can borrow your grandmother's handkerchief for your touchdown purse. A less stylish but equally effective option is a damp paper towel from your tailgate or the stadium restroom.

✔ **Smile:** When all else fails, put on some gloss and SMILE!

Accessory Checklist:

✔ Ticket	✔ Sunscreen
✔ Lip Gloss	✔ Cash
✔ Small Team-Logo Face Tattoo	✔ Great attitude!
✔ Camera	

Extra Point:

To take off your face tattoo before work on Monday morning, simply apply soap, warm water, and a washcloth to your face. Repeat as necessary. If my team wins, I usually leave it on through the airport the next day!

What's the Sexiest Thing a Belle Can Wear to a Football Game?

Gents Say

"Gotta rock the orange and blue sundress with the tattoo on the cheek. Can't beat it with a stick." **Pat Manning, Auburn.**

"Girls of the SEC look great in whatever they wear to the game." **Jack Porco, Kentucky**

"A nice black or red dress." **Alex Bray, Georgia**

"A houndstooth sundress." **Joe Whitt, III Alabama**

"A sundress in her favorite team's colors." **Florida Fan**

"Sundress. Never, EVER, wear jeans and a t-shirt." **Ole Miss Fan**

"Any Belle who wears a sundress that revolves around her team colors is a keeper. I want a Southern Belle who is not afraid to look pretty to watch a not-so-pretty sport. But most importantly, the sexiest thing a belle can wear is a positive attitude." **Calhoun Hipp, III South Carolina**

"Cowgirl boots and sundress." **Russ Allen, Vanderbilt**

"Her enthusiasm." **Warren Kroges, Tennessee**

"A dress with team colors (if the dress or purse can carry bourbon, huge plus)."
James Stozier, Auburn

"Jersey tailored to her figure and small bottoms." **Ryan Horton, Georgia**

"Sundress or jeggings and small jersey. Completely different but equally sexy."
Brandon Hudspeth, Ole Miss

"Face tattoo." **Clay Harris, LSU**

"Nothing particular; a Southern lady cheering on an SEC team is sexy enough!"
Michael Hart, Florida

"If the guy and the girl are from different schools it can be incredibly sexy for the girl to wear something in support of the guy's school. Of course, no one expects her to change allegiances, but in the appropriate setting, nothing can top seeing your girl in your school's colors. Notably, this should probably work both ways. There is nothing wrong with a guy showing support, again in the appropriate setting, for his girl's school – as long as there isn't some serious rivalry involved."
Charles Preuter, Alabama

"Anything she wants, if she is a Belle. As long as it's not so fashionable that it's painfully slow for walking to and from the tailgate and game; or makes her complain about not having a great time."
Ralls Rinch, Auburn

"Sundress and big sunglasses, party cup with booze in hand." **TJ Navarro, LSU**

A Winning Tailgating Strategy

Hosting a Championship Tailgate

How did Saturdays in Dixie become the most revered Saturdays in the country? It's simple: down here, we enjoy sharing heirloom recipes with kin and friends at our homes, our motor homes, or our motor vehicles, starting on Wednesday, for a Saturday game. Tailgating is an art form of hard work and dedication, a source of pride and some of a Southerner's greatest memories. In other words, tailgating is the pulse of the football-loving South.

No quarterback takes a snap without a play in mind; no Belle should host a tailgate without a game plan! Inevitably things will change, and you will have to be flexible, but with the help of this book you'll be able to scramble better than quarterback Tim Tebow.

Anyone can tailgate with SEC caliber by following the checklist below and adding a personal touch. Of course, you can always throw beers in a cooler or burgers on the grill, but this is the SEC. You have 80,000 of your closest friends coming over, so I don't recommend it!

Extra Point:

"Calling an audible from the line" is a term that means the players will figure everything out once they get to the line of scrimmage and "call" the play audibly. If your date or other Belles are giving you a hard time during the preparations for the tailgate or bad weather is looming, this is a good time to say, "We'll just have to call an audible from the line."

Top Five Tailgating Tips:

- Have a game plan and come prepared. No team takes the field without a game plan; you can't host a successful tailgate without some Xs and Os. Think through the menu, seating and supplies.

- The more the merrier. Southern hospitality applies now more than ever. You want an inviting tailgate where friends and strangers stop by. Offer a drink and some delectable snacks.

- Show your spirit. Do your homework on your team and its opponent so you can join the conversation with your guests. Use the tips from "Cramming for Conversation" *(see page 51)* to help!

- Clean up. Be respectful at home and away games. Next year the same game will be at your "home."

- Have another one! Once you start and get the hang of it, it's hard to stop. Invite friends to co-host; planning is half the fun!

Your Indispensable Tailgating Checklist:

Tape and tent

Use tape (string or ribbon also works) to rope off your lot the night before the game, then pop up your team-colored tent the morning of! You certainly can tailgate without a tent, but what outdoor living room isn't better without some shade, shelter, and structure?

Extra Point:

All schools have different rules for when and how you save tailgating spots.
Be sure to check the rules and get there early; it's worth it!

Wheels

No, not a car-wheels on your cooler, wheels on your dolly, wheels on
a wagon, wheels on a grill. Incorporate wheels whenever possible for
smoother tailgating transport. Lugging loads of team spirit without
wheels is as difficult as accepting your team's loss to your rival.

Chairs

Even the most seasoned tailgaters like a place to park every once in
a while. Your tailgate isn't going to look like your living room, but
it can be close! Bring your collection of stadium chairs and ask your
friends to bring some as well.

Extra Point:

I've collected a stadium chair for every game I've attended. This way, I always have a "special" chair for any fans that drop by!

Cooler

You can never have too many coolers. I suggest one for ice; one for beer, cokes and water; and one for food that needs to stay chilled (or warm). This may sound excessive, but coolers conveniently double as extra seats!

There are also coolers that keep things warm when plugged into your generator. This is helpful when you don't have chafing dishes and it's late in the season.

Ice

It may seem too obvious to put on this checklist, but forgetting ice could single-handedly ruin a tailgate. Always grab a few bags of ice on the morning of the tailgate to chill your cooler contents before you head to the party. When people ask what to bring, if there is any doubt, suggest ice! Serving warm beer and sweating in a sundress is not ideal for acting and looking like a Belle.

You can also save room by freezing water bottles. They serve as ice in the cooler and will be nice and cold after the game or late on the hot day.

Cups

SEC schools do not allow open containers. They essentially support being over-served, but require the refinery to drink out of a cup, not a bottle or can. Consider buying cups in bulk at the beginning of the season or, even better, personalize your own set of stadium cups.

Mrs. Campbell, a Southern Belle of Alabama roots and a Tennessee address, makes the world's best customized stadium cups and koozies. E-mail her at CarolsCustomCups@gmail.com and tell her I sent you. She's used to making personalized game day cups for me! Some of the axioms I have used on cups include:

Alabama: "If you want to walk the heavenly streets of gold, you have to know the password: 'Roll, Tide, Roll.'" - **Bear Bryant**

 Florida: "If you ain't a Gator, you must be Gator bait."

 Kentucky: "Tough girls come from New York. Sweet girls, they're from Georgia. But us Kentucky girls, we have fire and ice in our blood. We can ride horses, be debutantes, throw left hooks, and drink with the boys, all the while making sweet tea, darlin'. And if we have an opinion, you know you're gonna hear it." - **Ashley Judd**

 LSU: **"Geaux Tigers!"**

 MS State: "Hotty Toddy, gosh Almighty, when's Ole Miss goin' to be somebody?"

 Ole Miss: We may not win every game, but we've never lost a tailgate!"

 South Carolina: "God is smiling on South Carolina" - **Steve Spurrier**

 "When it's 4th and long, you can have the milk drinkers, and I'll take the whiskey drinkers every time." - **Max McGee**

Add the game and date to your cup if you plan to use it as a gift. Always include school colors and a football!

Paper Towels

Always have at least three rolls of paper towels accessible to you and your guests. To go for the extra point in a sticky situation, consider bringing baby wipes. If wipes aren't rugged enough for you, ice from a cooler and a paper towel should be able to take care of most tailgate messes.

Trash Bags

Bring plenty of big, black, durable trash bags. Belles are not those trashy people who leave behind a mess! Come prepared to tidy up. The more trash bags you have hanging on the pole of your tent, off of your hitch, or at the end of your table, the more people will use them, and the less you will have to pick up at the end.

Full bags either go in the back of your Suburban, the nearby dumpster, or remain in clear view for the pickup system.

Tunes

Thankfully, speakers have become smaller and more powerful, which is perfect for tailgating. Be sure to bring a set of cordless speakers compatible with your iPod. You don't need to host your own concert and intrude on your neighbor's tailgate, but a great playlist will keep your tailgate *the* place to be before kickoff.

Décor

Why work hard if you aren't going to take the time to properly display the fruits of your labor? Tupperware may be the best way to transport the pre-game grub, but it is not the preferred way to serve your prized recipes. Think Ole Miss. While not every school has The Grove and not every school competes over whose silver is shinier, you can achieve the same grandeur with affordable décor.

Always remember, flowers are as welcomed as front porch company. Be clean, organized and team-spirited. Bring your necessities and let your hospitality, charm and game-winning-recipes do the rest.

Extra Point:

Swoozie's, an exclusively Southern gift store, provides all of your needs for any theme at affordable prices, including football spreaders, team platters, gridiron chip bowls, referee wine holders, etc. Swoozie's loves football as much as we do and certainly knows what makes a good tailgate!

Table or Tailgate

You'll need somewhere to have your "bar" and buffet. You could use an actual truck's tailgate if your stadium allows, or you can invest in folding tables that are convenient and ever-so-classy.

When laying out a table, be sure to bring a team-colored tablecloth, matching plates and napkins. This is your opportunity to add flare. There is no such thing as too much team spirit. The tablecloth need not be starched cloth, but that little touch makes a big difference in your décor.

Add flower arrangements, football-shaped bowls, and dishes. Hang a team banner. If this is your one tailgate to host this season, why not go all out? One LSU fan put a real Gator head at her tailgate accompanied by local newspapers that had predicted a Tiger victory. Think Ole Miss class with LSU-style flare!

Extra Point:

You may add some higher-end items to your tailgate checklist. Keep in mind that these will raise you to the next level of commitment as a tailgater. If you decide to bring any of the items below, be prepared to stay posted at the tailgate for the entire game or to take the time to put them away before going into the stadium. If you decide to bring a generator, you might as well bring a fan to plug in. As far as tents, TVs and grills, the bigger the better!

- ✔ TV
- ✔ Grill
- ✔ Generator
- ✔ Fan
- ✔ Silver chafing dishes
- ✔ Mint Julep glasses
- ✔ Great Grandmother's Candelabras

MENU CHECKLIST

Remember, your guests are here for the football and the party, not the cuisine. That being said, the tastiness and convenience of your menu will make your tailgate outshine any in the lot.

Blitz-Bites

Your guests will want to take a couple of trips through your buffet to fill up on your game day fare. As a Belle hostess you should provide a nice spread of dips, bite-sized protein, and lots of desserts! Keep in mind, no one, especially we Belles, wants to feel full and bloated after eating. Offer some healthy options for your guests who are trying to watch their Belle-ish figures.

Don't feel obligated to provide a seven-course meal. Simply give people a nice variety of your game day culinary talent. Include one main dish, a few sides, and offer them a drink. After all, you do have pre-game interviews to watch and a game to attend!

Hydrate

Whether you're at the legal age to enjoy a bourbon or prefer water on game day, a seasoned Belle will offer a variety of non-alcoholic drinks and libations for her guests. I don't suggest bourbon if you are trying to stay cool, but then again, when has the SEC ever catered to the faint of heart? If you are willing to get creative, which makes for more fun, think of drinks that are the same color as your team.

Extra Point:

Lois "Hon" Truss, raised in Luverne, AL but now resides in Birmingham, happens to be an Alabama fan in an Auburn family who annually hosts the Iron Bowl game at her Birmingham home. She scores serious extra points by flying in Tiger beer from China and buying Elephant beer from the local liquor store! She caters to her team and her family while impressing guests. A true Gridiron Belle!

Equipment Room: (where to purchase your game day "equipment")

- Swoozie's
- Local correspondence and gift Shops
- Target's "dollar bins"
- Campus bookstores
- Local grocery stores

Equipment:

- School or football-themed platters and bowls
- Team-colored or branded cups
- Disposable tablecloth
- Team flag
- Flowers

Tailgate Bin:

A tailgate bin, invented by Tennessee and Ole Miss tailgate experts Pam Richardson and Nina Dyer, keeps all of your smaller, yet necessary, tailgate gear nearby. Store this bin under the table and keep it hidden by using a long tablecloth that drapes to the ground. This is the equivalent of your first-aid kit. Beneath the tablecloth you can stash everything you need for any situation. By the way, it's probably not a bad idea to have an actual first-aid kit nearby!

Here are a few items to get your tailgate bin started:

- Foil
- Clorox Wet Wipes
- Fabric for tablecloth
- Breath mints
- Ziploc bags
- Lightbulb candles
- Sharp knife
- Bottle opener
- Backup box of cookies and crackers
- Flashlight
- Advil
- Extra trash bags
- Backup batteries
- Extension cord
- Extra pair of flat shoes
- Matches
- Extra paper goods (plates, napkins, etc.) and plastic utensils
- Emergency decorations (team shakers, beads, and any school-themes trinkets)

> To keep food piping hot, heat a few granite tiles in the oven, then wrap them in a towel and place them in a "cooler." Keep all hot items together in one container for best results.

Extra Point:

Belles, we all know that we are perfectly capable of carrying coolers, lugging trash to a dumpster, lighting a grill, starting a generator, and getting our own drinks. But, we also know that our dates don't get manicures, they usually have an extra shirt in the car, and have likely worked out their biceps slightly harder than we have. Why risk breaking into a glisten before absolutely necessary? Not to mention, since we are getting better at calling plays and penalties, we better let them still feel like manly men on game day!

What is Your Favorite Gameday Tradition?

Belles Say

"Pre-tailgating festivities on Dickson Street and then tailgating." **Carrie Linden, Arkansas**

"Tailgating at UT was sensational. You became best friends with the people who were next to your spot, and you were just as crazy about UT football as the person next to you. Literally crazy; I mean you have not experienced a football game until you walk into Neyland Stadium. Not only is it huge, but we have fans willing to risk their lives to fill it up. That is just the way it goes down in the Volunteer State." **Shelley Tasman, Tennessee**

"Dawg Walk with all players and coaches." **Amanda Richmond, Mississippi State**

"The FOOD! I love to walk from tailgate to tailgate, tasting all of the yummy treats!"
Elizabeth Bordelon Adams, LSU

"Watching the Eagle fly. It always makes me tear up and gives me a sense of pride."
Peyton Gregory, Auburn

"Singing the Rammer Jammer cheer after winning a game." **Beth Erickson, Alabama**

"In the unlikely event of a noon game, SAE puts on 'Screw your Breakfast' complete with silver champagne mimosa fountains." **Janie Walker, Kentucky**

"Dressing up." **Carrie Fusi, Georgia**

Home Field Advantage:
Tailgating in Your Living Room

Hosting a game day watch party at your home is all of the pleasure, half of the hassle. The overarching theme stays the same: fun, friends, and football. Whether you are hosting five or fifty people to watch the big game, fun will be had by all if you follow these guidelines:

Provide ample seating
Comfort is important for a four-hour game. Make sure you have arranged or rearranged your furniture for optimal seating. Some people may have to sit on the floor, but the more chairs or couches, the better. For especially large parties, you might even put sofas on bed risers, which you can find anywhere that sells dorm-room gear, to create stadium seating.

Bring out the Gridiron grub
Having access to your entire kitchen means you can step up the excellence of the usual pigskin fare. Try a recipe that is delicious but too complicated to haul to a tailgate. Even if you decide to serve full dinner at halftime, keep some snacks out for the first and second halves.

Go all out with the décor
Since your tailgating décor is likely stored at your home, you've never had easier access to your team's colors. Make sure your flag is waving proudly, your tablecloths match, and the team paraphernalia that you've collected over the years is proudly displayed. If you can't be at the stadium, bring the flare of the stadium to you!

Hit the lights
It may sound odd, but the lighting at your watch party makes a difference. If it's a night game, switch off the overhead lights and turn on the lamps; you could even light a fire. If you're hosting a day game, open the blinds and perhaps even the door.

Make sure you're equipped

If you can count the number of guests on both hands, it is okay to have just one large TV. If you have more guests than fingers, strongly consider a second or third TV. This will mitigate any tension that may rise between serious and less serious fans. If weather and space permit, setting up a second or third TV outdoors will have your guests raving about the party!

Host Etiquette

The number of guests will vary. Always be prepared for a few more and expect a few no-shows. Your role as host at a home watch party is the same as always: Greet your guests, offer them their first drink, show them where the food is, tell them where the bathroom is, ask about their mama, make introductions, and walk guests to the door when they leave — if it's not during OT or a fourth down. You're also responsible for replenishing the snacks, but you are not responsible for high entertainment in the form of excessive conversation. After all, you're having a party because you want to watch the game!

Guest Etiquette

If you RSVP, show up. Be sure to ask the hosts what you can bring to contribute to snacks, drinks, or ambiance. If there is no specific instruction, an appetizer or dessert is always welcome, as well as team-colored flowers for the host. (Make sure the flowers are already in a vase so you don't take the hostess away from her hosting duties or the game—but you already knew that.) As a guest, mingle with other fans, pour your own drinks, and be sure to compliment the hostess on her divine game day treats. Yep, you guessed it; a thank-you note is also in order!

Extra Point:

Think twice about hosting a big watch party if your team is playing. As a hostess, you'll be pulled in several directions to fulfill hosting duties and will be distracted from many plays. If you're the type of Belle who cannot miss a single snap, go ahead and pass on hosting duties for that week's game! I learned this the hard way when I combined the National Championship and a "book completion party" on the same night. Thankfully, Auburn still won!

Mama Says,
"Never Show Up Empty-Handed"

Showing up to a watch party or a game weekend stay without a hostess gift would be like wearing jeans and a t-shirt to an Ole Miss game: it's just not right. Like your ticket to the game, a hostess gift simply cannot be overlooked. Nor should you purchase one thirty minutes before kickoff! The key is to let your hostess know that you appreciate her warm hospitality. Just as she's not skimping on the food and drinks, don't skimp on the thoughtfulness of her gift!

To avoid breaking the ultimate Southern guest law, keep some of these gifts on hand. Some require more thoughtful planning than others, but that's what we Belles are known for, right?

Here are some great go-to options:

- *Gridiron Belles: A Guide to Saturdays in Dixie*
- Team logo or colored napkins
- Team Tervis Tumblers
- Team- or football—themed platters
- Football-themed tea towels
- Bibs, bows and socks (if the hostess has little fans in training)
- Personalized stadium cups from Mrs. Campbell (see page 79)
- Tailgate cookie bouquet (Send ahead)
- School/football ornament (Great for bowl season)
- Flowers (Send ahead of time; these can be called in from the airport, if need be)
- Bottle of bourbon with his/her family name on it

- Handmade cross-stitch (not last minute, but very thoughtful)
- Homemade delicatessen accompanied with the recipe for your host to enjoy when you leave!

If you're facing an emergency, and I mean a *true* emergency, such as losing the rights to your season tickets or learning that your daughter is getting kicked out of the Chi-O house, you may send a gift with your thank-you note. But try your darndest to deliver a gridiron treat upon your anticipated arrival!

Where to find hostess gifts:

- Gridiron Belles Book, **www.gridironbelles.com**
- Team napkins, plates, platters, tea towels, **www.swoozies.com**
- Tervis Tumblers, **www.tervistumbler.com**
- Personalized stadium cups, **CarolsCustomCups@gmail.com**
- School or football ornament, individual school bookstore and websites or local shops in your area

Belles on a Budget

Despite our loyalty, fans don't make commission. We must show our allegiance out of our own pockets, which can get pretty pricey pretty quickly!

Just because you are the most creative and organized tailgater in your group, the financial burden should not fall squarely on your pretty shoulders.

Here's how to tailgate on a dime (or at least, on a quarter):

- Invite others to co-host with you. You can split the costs and have twice the fun.

- Potlucks are the easiest and cheapest ways to enjoy your Saturday whether you are at the game or in front of the flat screen.

- Décor can be pricey, but not if you're creative! Wrap old paper grocery bags around a potted mum and tie a pretty ribbon or raffia in your team's colors around it.

- No need to splurge on dry cleaning your linens; burlap makes for affordable tablecloths and adds to the rugged football feel of the fall. Just ask the fabric store to cut it to your dimensions and pull some string off the edges for a rustic fray.
  (Tip: Do this outdoors; it gets messy.)

- Also suggested: gingham in team colors or fabrics with team logos are sometimes available and very affordable!

Save time and money on recipes:

- Fried chicken from KFC, Chick-Fil-A, or Bojangles is cheaper than frying it on the spot Beer is cheaper than liquor.

🏈 Forget expensive bakery goods—a box of MoonPies is as Southern as it gets. Straight from Chattanooga, the original marshmallow sandwich is a must at your tailgate when you're trying to save—and even when you're not!

🏈 People still love pizza. If hosting at home, go ahead and call The Papa.

Once a Tailgater, Always a Tailgater

If you know you'll be hosting or co-hosting more than once this season (and next), go ahead and stock up on supplies at the beginning of the season. Head to your favorite bulk store and purchase the oversized bag of red-and-white forks or purple-and-yellow plates and napkins. If you have a garage or large pantry, then by all means, purchase your favorite chips, brownie mix or frozen burgers in bulk (not the best for taste, but not bad for the price).

Turning Too Late Into Early Enough

When it's too late to purchase football paraphernalia for one season, it's usually the perfect time to stock up for next season. Think like a candy-craving shopper the day after Halloween—as soon as the season is over, take advantage of the sales on your team's colors, tablecloths and everything else you you'll need next fall. Enjoy your off-season knowing you've saved!

Extra Point:

Keep a plastic bin stocked with tailgating essentials and all your football toys and refurbish as necessary. Consider decorating this bin with team colors, logos, and your name on top of the lid.

You Can't Put a Price on Etiquette:

A Belle knows that even when she's on a budget, she doesn't expect anything for free. If you cannot afford to contribute the tenderloin for the tailgate, show up with two bags of ice, a simple recipe, a home team program or your camera, and a single team-colored flower for your host. You can even bring a "Game Day Playlist" to give the gift of team spirit through song. Just be sure that when you do finally encounter that windfall down the road, you do some proper, spirit-filled hosting!

Dissing With Class–
The Dos and Don'ts of
Insulting Your Opponent

As Belles, we know the game. We also know that SEC football is all about having fun with friendly (and occasionally not-so-friendly) competition, so we don't get too wrapped up in pre- and post-game slights.

Suffice it to say, unless you really know your stats and facts, you should leave the trash-talking to someone else. Before you embarrass yourself by telling every Mississippi State fan that your Vandy 'Dores are going to out-run, out-tackle and outscore the Bulldogs, follow these zinger guidelines:

Get your facts straight. There is not a weaker (or more embarrassing) insult than one that is factually inaccurate. Study up before you dish it out and avoid tasting vinegar.

Wait until you win. Bragging about your team's talent is great. Eating the foot in your mouth after you lose is not.

Payback is... well, you know. Be prepared to withstand a counterattack (even from kids), especially if your trash-talking earned you nothing more than a big loss. Being an SEC fan means you need to have thick skin.

Lock it up when you lose. You lost. Your bowl-game dreams were just shattered, but shhh… your insults are no longer relevant. You can always blame an injured quarterback, a loud stadium, an unexpected torrential downpour, coaching breakdowns, poor officiating, or a young team. Or, you can just take the highroad and go back to tailgating and get geared up for next week.

Use your words. Four-letter words are easy to find after four quarters of bourbon. Such vocabulary lacks the desired wit and charm that makes us Southerners great. Even worse, the little ones will copy your lead, and we know chillins will pick up their own four-letter words when the time is right. Keep your digs clean and aim them at the team or the officials.

When in doubt… When you have absolutely nothing else to say, proclaim that the other team cheats. They probably do.

Extra Point:

If you are running your mouth about your team, don't expect your date to stand up for you when people throw insults back. This happened at an Alabama game when an Auburn Belle was dishing it out. When the Alabama fans responded with sharp insults aimed at Cam Newton (the Auburn quarterback at the time), she got so upset she asked her boyfriend to step in. Only problem was, he was a BAMA fan. And he knew that asking an Alabama fan not to talk smack about Auburn's Heisman-winning quarterback is like asking a Belle not to put on makeup for a game. Shugah, there is no force on earth that can stop it.

Loving the Gridiron

It's no secret that many Gents look forward to *game day* with the same passion and anticipation that many Belles look forward to their *wedding* day. Gents from Kentucky to Georgia and every land of Dixie in between know their entire season is at risk with the phrase "fall wedding." Perfect fall weather also means that you will inevitably be getting married on game day, forcing you to share some of your spotlight with rivalries, upsets, and BCS rankings.

I'll confess, two of my pledge sisters who happen to be well-versed Gridiron Belles had their weddings smack dab in the middle of season. We all survived. Barely, but we did. So I'm not cruel enough to suggest eliminating fall nuptials altogether. Just do me and everyone else in your wedding a favor. Embrace our inner fandom by following the suggestions below.

What's a Belle to do?

For starters, get your nuptials off on the right cleat by setting a date in the spring (recruiting season is less of an excuse for a Gent with commitment phobia).

After all, isn't wedded bliss all about compromise? Sure it is; so long as it's not the compromise of your team allegiance.

Extra Point:

If you are engaged to a guy who is willing to get married in the fall, he may not care about SEC football like you do. Consider the possibility that he is not the right one for you.

Your Game Day Wedding Playbook

If you must marry between the months of September and January, follow these simple rules:

- ✔ Check the schedule. No wedding during rival games or home games is permitted. Period. Please?

- ✔ There are only seven weeks of home football; enjoy every single one of them, because the longest season out there is non-football season.

- ✔ Away games are less painful, but try to schedule your big day for an off weekend.

- ✔ If you and your groom do not cheer for the same team, be sure to check the schedules of both teams.

What to expect if you have a Gridiron Belle wedding:

Be prepared. Many Mississippi weddings have guests, usually of the elderly male status, who wear earpieces that broadcast the game during the ceremony and reception. I'm not saying it's right; I'm saying it happens.

Expect invitation regrets from your family members and close friends, especially if they are diehard fans.

While "happily ever after" is still the primary focus, be prepared for guests to give you a congratulatory hug while also flashing their iPhones, full of scores, to the groom.

Add a note in the program, "Thank you for being with us on our wedding day and game day. We appreciate your love and support of us and your teams. Please use your electronic devices to regularly update the bride and groom on the scores *after* the ceremony!"

Show your spirit, but keep it classy. While matching your bridesmaid dresses to your team's uniforms is a short distance between spirited and obsessive, some sign of your spirit in the form of a groom's cake, napkin colors, and party favors are welcome fun! Some Gridiron Belle weddings feature the fight song of either the bride or groom's school as the two leave the church for the first time as husband and wife!

A Checklist of Topics to Cover with Your Wedding Planner:

✔ Most weddings have a cocktail hour. This is the perfect time to let your guests indulge in the games before dinner and dancing.

✔ Arrange for TVs to be available for your guests, your new husband, and you. Personalize a small room or area in your team's colors, and embrace the idea that some of your guests will be more interested in watching the Vandy - Tennessee game than in watching you dance with your flower girl.

✔ Have your wedding coordinator keep an eye on the scores and give them to the band every once in a while, so they can make a fun announcement to the crowd right before they break into "Sweet Home Alabama."

✔ Have the drink butler provide an updated list of scores that he can share every fifteen minutes while he's handing out drinks.

✔ Make the reception's signature cocktail reminiscent of your game day drink of choice.

✔ It's a no-brainer: make sure the band learns your fight song! If you are marrying a rival, be sure to play both songs and be thoughtful enough to learn your new spouse's lyrics as well!

✔ Make a wooden cut-out of your favorite coach, mascot, or your teams' jerseys available at a photo station for pictures to be taken and used as favors!

✔ Use shakers in place of rice or sparklers for the send-off.

A note about accommodating your guests and fans:

If you want your wedding day or night to be all eyes on you, by all means, keep TVs and announcements out of your plans. But these days, smart phones can stream the games live. Unless you want your guests hovering on top of one another to watch the game in the men's lounge (which is right where I would also be— no offense), try some of the above. Most people will have their fill during cocktail hour and will be delighted to share in your evening of "happily every-season after."

Vows, Visitors, and Victory:
Hosting a Wedding Shower During the Fall

If you are responsible for throwing a wedding shower during our beloved football season, you're in luck. Forget a "Stock the Bar" party—make it a tailgate! The idea behind this party is to unite the couple and celebrate their teams as well as their love. Your fiancé and his comrades aren't going to say "no" to an amazing tailgate or game day party, and the Belles aren't going to say "no" to a shower where the Gents are actually excited to be there.

Aside from the spirited environments of the SEC tailgating hotspots, there is no better place for a theme party than the comfort of your own home, complete with a full kitchen, multiple TVs, trashcans, bathrooms, and air conditioning.

Of course, you'll need more than the basics for this little shindig. Here you'll find a list of must-haves and added-bonuses for hosting a football shower at a stadium or at home. In all of your planning and execution, consider the bride and groom's infatuation with their teams, especially if their teams happen to be rivals.

EQUIPMENT:

Tents & Tailgates:

All standard tailgating equipment applies (*see Tailgating Check-List, page 77*) plus the extra point equipment. This is a special day, so bring out all the bells and whistles! You absolutely should not host this tailgate party without the following:

- Flat screen TV
- Plenty of chairs
- Table space for gifts
- Music
- Excessively stocked bar
- Delicious food

Living Room Huddle:

- Two flat-screen TVs, no less than 42 inches, to create two "stadiums"

- Chairs, couches, and open space (rearrange your furniture if necessary to make the viewing area more spacious)

- Gift area with team-colored tablecloth

Etiquette Tip:

As a guest, feel free to sneak off to "stadium number two" to watch the game, but only after you have greeted the happy couple and the host. Even then, you and your date should not sit by yourselves; invite other obsessed fans to come with you. Between quarters and at halftime, you are expected to socialize.

DÉCOR:

Tents & Tailgates:

- Support the team and the couple by customizing for the bride and groom. If it's a mixed marriage, be sure that half of the tent is in her team colors and half is in his. Think "equal closet space" until the SEC Championship Game.

- Stadium cups with the couple's name on them are a great way to unite the couple, despite the rivalry. The cups make great takeaways for guests.

- Have a banner or a sign made to hang on your tent. You may even want to add balloons. The sign will help your guests find your party. Fellow fans will also stop by to wish them luck for the game and the marriage.

Living Room Huddle:

Décor ideas from the outdoor tailgate-shower still apply, but with a nicer touch.

Team colored tablecloths or a gridiron-green cloth add a stadium feel.

Shine your silver and press your linens. Remember that this isn't just an SEC football party; it's a shower honoring the couple.

Accent with fresh flowers (team colors, of course), cold pint glasses for beer, and real champagne flutes.

Personalize M&Ms in team colors* with the couple's monogram on them. The leftovers are a nice take-home gift for the bride and groom.

Display pictures of the couple and their friends from previous tailgates and games for a personal touch.

LET THE GAMES BEGIN

Much to the satisfaction of the male guests (and some Belles), traditional wedding shower games are as welcome as Big 12 fans— unless the games are tailgate games or include putting money on the spread. Take your pick from the suggestions below.

Tents & Tailgates:

Cornhole, washers, and golf (the tailgate game; although a small putting green isn't a bad idea) are welcome at tailgates. Have couples enter into a tournament, with the honored couple getting an automatic bid to the final game.

Leave all other shower games for less football-themed gatherings. People still want to tailgate without organized activities. Plus, the real game will be here soon enough!

Living Room Huddle:

Again, traditional shower games will be omitted, minus one at halftime.

During halftime, ask the couple to answer a series of questions to see how well each knows the other's football preferences. Get creative! Here are a few samples to get you started:

Who is his/her favorite SEC quarterback?"

"Would she wear impractical heels or practical flats to a rival game?"

"What's his/her favorite game-day ritual?"

"When was he the most upset about a bad call? Tell us the story!"

"What is the first game he/she ever attended?"

"Who is the commentator he quotes the most?"

"What is the most historically significant game he/she has attended?"

"Which stadium does he/she favor?"

"Which SEC coach does she/he most despise?"

"How would he or she respond to missing the (enter favorite team's largest rival game) for work, family, or friends?"

Before or after the game, if weather and space permit, start a game of cornhole or horseshoes outside and some friendly, legal betting inside.

ROSTER:

Tents & Tailgates:

In unison, Belles: "The more the merrier!" This is a tailgate, after all. Invite the fans on the bride and groom's list (E-vite or Paperless Post are perfect and have football-themed layouts), and then spread the word by mouth. Encourage other acquaintances to stop by to help toast the love of the couple and SEC football.

Cell phones rarely work on game day close to the stadium. Be sure to give accurate directions to your tailgate ahead of time. Include street intersections, school buildings, parking lot numbers, tent section, and what your sign says. You don't want the best man or mother of the bride to miss this event!

People will have their own teams' games to attend in a neighboring state, but if invited early enough, you'll be surprised how even the most dedicated fans will make a visit to a rival stadium if a close friend is hosting a tailgate.

Extra Point:

You are not responsible for acquiring game tickets for everyone. Some guests will have season tickets or will do what they can to scalp tickets; some will not. As host, you or one of your co-hosts should plan on staying at the tailgate to accompany guests (and keep an eye on the flatscreen) throughout the game.

Living Room Huddle:

Your list of invitees depends on both the amount of space you have and on the people with whom the bride and groom wish to share this special day.

Many card stores have football-themed invitations, or you can send a very SEC-friendly E-vite, depending on your budget.

The gift theme of the party, football, should be clear on the invitation.

Request an RSVP so you can prepare accordingly.

Provide accurate directions, along with a cell phone number and land-line (if applicable) in case fans get lost. I assure you, no one wants to miss this party!

GRIDIRON GRUB:

Tents & Tailgates:

Since Belles always provide enough food to feed the team, it won't be the slightest bit of an inconvenience to share game-changing treats with everyone who stops by.

Special occasions tend to bring larger crowds, so keep it simple and festive. Limit yourself to one or two hearty items, one or two appetizers, and a few desserts.

If you've been wanting to bring those chaffing dishes out for tailgating, this is the time!

Use team colors and monograms whenever possible.

Living Room Huddle:

A full kitchen offers the luxury of a plethora of gametime crowd pleasers that are a little fancier than many tailgating options.

If the game is at night, go for a heartier spread, such as gumbo, ribs, or tenderloin.

For a mid-afternoon game, heavy pick-up food is perfectly acceptable.

Do as much of the cooking as you can ahead of time, so that you can socialize with your guests instead of getting stuck in the kitchen.

Don't forget to put out snacks by that second or third TV. Just because the viewers are serious, anti-social, and obsessed, it doesn't mean they aren't hungry!

Gifts:

Gifts for this shower should be, you guessed it, team-themed. A few ideas to consider:

Platters with team colors and mascots

Team-specific Tervis Tumblers

Team cover for the game day grill

Personalized stadium cups with announcements like "Mary Leigh and Caldwell's Tailgate in the Grove"

Elegant ice bucket

The idea is to provide the honored couple with nice, updated team paraphernalia so that they can host their own game day parties as a new couple (hopefully joined in support of *one* team).

If it's a house divided, be courteous. You might bring something small for each, give a gift to the person you are closer to, or make the soon-to-be spouse feel welcome by honoring his or her team in light of your own loyalties. Remember, a Belle always gives a gift that she would want to receive.

No one can ever have too many treasures for his or her team!

Tents & Tailgates:

Bringing gifts to an outdoor event can be cumbersome for the honored guests. If the host or honored couple lives nearby and festivities are planned at their home before or after the game, you should drop off the gifts there. If this is not possible, do the couple a favor and ship the gift directly to their home. Bring a congratulatory card to the tailgate.

As a host, be sure to have the couple's most up-to-date address available.

If you want your gift to be used during the tailgate, coordinate with the host. Personalized platters and stadium cups can be helpful at the tailgate and are easily transported back to the car during clean up.

Living Room Huddle:

If you're a guest, feel free to give more elaborate and creative gifts when the shower is at someone's home. A few suggestions to keep in mind:

A basket overflowing with Volunteer orange cocktail napkins, a football bottle opener, a set of Ole Miss coasters, a Gator cheese platter, and a copy of *Gridiron Belles* makes for a wonderful gift for any fan.

A monogrammed Mint Julep cup with the couple's name, the date, and their team's favorite saying (e.g., "Hotty Toddy," "Roll Tide," "Geaux Tigers," etc.). Is there anything more Southern?

Extra Point:

My favorite LSU fan, Lauren Bordelon, once gave me a hand-painted Auburn platter. Not only do I use it every game day, and even during the off-season, but it's a gift that is truly one of a kind!

STRENGTH OF SCHEDULE (SETTING THE DATE!):

Choose your weekend carefully. Make sure the bride and groom don't have plans to go to a game and that there are some good rival games being played. Team schedules are released sometimes years in advance, so with a little research you can find the perfect weekend. A night game will create a different atmosphere than a day game, so be ready to host accordingly.

Tents & Tailgates:

Four to five hours before kickoff (often even earlier) is the fairly standard time for tailgating. If you decide to start earlier or later, spread the word by phone or e-mail the week before.

If your guests are coming in from out of town, game-time is less of an issue, because everyone is already coming to the game, regardless of kickoff time.

Living Room Huddle:

The airtime for the game is generally not announced until one or two weeks beforehand. Consequently, TV dictates the start time for your party, too.

Start early anyway. Get on people's calendars for the game. When the TV schedule comes out, send a follow up e-mail or make calls to announce the kickoff time for your party.

Be open to turning this day into an open house if you're up for it.

Hosting for a day game will likely leave you hosting for a night game as well, so be prepared!

Gridiron Shower Etiquette:
A BRIEF RUNDOWN

The bride and groom are still the guests of honor;
act accordingly, despite the rivalry on the field.

Consider making your host's gift something that relates to
his or her team. He or she clearly loves football too!

Leave all opponent hostility elsewhere. This is a celebratory event,
despite your team's performance, so be sure to keep smiling even
after that terrible interception.

Mingle with the other teams, at least for the day.

Contribute to atmosphere, conversation, and general enjoyment.
Don't pitch a fit if you can't watch every down; rather, thank the
SEC gods that you are able to see any down.

If you're going to gossip excessively during the fourth quarter or on
third-and-long about wedding plans, please do not be near the TV!

Unless the hosts encourage you to stay for another game, go ahead
and make your exit after the game for which you were invited.

Send a thank-you note. This will likely be the most fun you and
your date ever have at a couple's shower. So much so, that your date
may even feel inclined to write the note to the host!

Saturdays in Dixie

We simply love when a sweet, soft, Southern Belle cheers in front of a Yankee at the top of her lungs for her team or in disbelief about the ref's call. Yankees think they've landed on Mars—but it's probably just Mississippi or Louisiana.

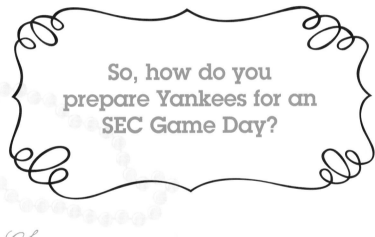

So, how do you prepare Yankees for an SEC Game Day?

Belles Say

"Don't associate with Yankees." **Morgan Roussel Volion, Auburn**

" 'Y'all' is singular. 'All y'all is plural. 'All y'all's' is plural possessive." **Kentucky Fan**

I think you just need to tell them to overdress and come with an empty belly. " **Elizabeth Bordelon Adams, LSU**

It's all about the Southern hospitality. Ladies, first, you have to lose the hair gel, get a Polo, and learn to like cheap beer." **Shelley Tasman, Tennessee**

"Lots of fratty, drunk kids." **Cathleen Leonard, Georgia**

"I don't really do a lot of preparing 'cause I like to see their natural reaction when they realize how intense it is." **Amanda Richmond, Mississippi State**

"I tell the guys to bring a pair of chinos and a button-down, and I tell the girls to bring a dress and have a drink. The rest will all play out." **Janie Walker, Kentucky**

"I am a Yankee. I'm from New York. So it's easy for me to translate, but nothing could ever fully prepare you. All you have to remember is to leave your inhibitions behind!"
Lindsay Morgan, Tennessee

"There is no way to prepare them. You just tell them about it, and they look at you like you're crazy." **Carrie Fusi, Georgia**

"I assess the Yankee's level of respect for the SEC before extending an invite to a game. If they pass this initial test, I usually share some of my favorite game day stories. I also send them articles about the two teams that are playing and about the tailgating experience at the school where the game will be played. I always address appropriate attire and behavior. "
Beth Erickson, Alabama

"Get lots of rest!" **Carrie Linden, Arkansas**

"Go shopping." **Kailyn Aertker, Ole Miss**

"Just warn them that it's more fun than they ever had tailgating at their college."
Kelly Golson, Georgia

"I let them experience it for themselves because it's hard to explain." **Julie Foster, Tennessee**

We drink Coke, not 'pop.'" **Vanderbilt Fan**

It's like having a backyard cookout with 86,000 of your closest friends." **Peyton Gregory, Auburn**

"Tell them they will be up earlier on a Saturday than most; they will not get tired (even if they are), and prepare them for lots and lots of crazy fans that live and die for their team."
Kelly Goddard, Florida

Dress code is extremely important. You will stick out if you don't dress according to code."
Jeanie Sleadd, Alabama

Dress them in red and black, and make sure that they're okay with the fact that they'll be drinking heavily before noon." **Claire Theilman, Georgia**

The Southeastern Conference

While there are only 10 Commandments, to be a true Gridiron Belle, you need to know the 12 false (or maybe real) idols of SEC football teams. The SEC is made up of an Eastern and Western Division, each with six teams. Ladies, commit these teams to memory like you would your favorite designers. They are:

SEC (Southeastern Conference)

EASTERN DIVISION	WESTERN DIVISION
Florida	Alabama
Georgia	Arkansas
Kentucky	Auburn
South Carolina	LSU
Tennessee	Mississippi
Vanderbilt	Mississippi State

How It All Started:

The game of football as we now know it took root in 1869 with the Rutgers-Yale game in Newark, New Jersey. Even though it was tardy to the party, the outstanding idea to create the SEC happened in 1932.

At inception, the SEC consisted of thirteen teams: Alabama, Auburn, Florida, Georgia, Georgia Tech, Kentucky, LSU, Mississippi, Mississippi State, Tennessee, Tulane, Sewanee, and Vanderbilt. Sewanee left the SEC first in 1940 to allow athletes to focus more on academics. Georgia Tech seceded in 1964 and Tulane in 1966. It wasn't until 1991 that the SEC expanded and invited two other Southern states, Arkansas and South Carolina, to compete in the proudest conference membership of the South.

Divided into east and west divisions, the winners of each division play one other in the SEC Championship game, which is held at the end of each season at the Georgia Dome in Atlanta.

University of Alabama

Maybe it's the extraordinary tailgating on The Quad. Perhaps it's Bear Bryant's looming legacy. It could be the thousands of shakers that move vigorously for four hours straight during a game.   Whatever the reason, The University of Alabama has mastered the SEC football experience. Love or hate the Tide, you have to respect their brilliance; hype and animated diehards are in every corner, regardless of where you pop-up your tent in Tuscaloosa.

For the full BAMA experience, take a walk down Paul Bryant Drive or sip a Yellow Hammer with friends in The Quad or on The Strip. Whatever you do, be sure to pay your respect to The Bear; stop by his statue and museum, or just wear houndstooth.

What's the unspoken dress code when attending the greatest football experience in the South? It's similar to preparing for senior prom, only there's more pressure—and this event happens six or seven times per year. Around here, the competition is more intense than the cheerleading captain running for homecoming queen. Belles come from all over the state to compete to be Belle of the tailgate!

Show up prepared with short fancy black and crimson dresses, straight hair, and high (high) heels. Top it all off with the best accessory: an attitude that says you were handpicked by the football angels.

If it will complete your outfit, take the liberty to wear red, instead of crimson. Any elephant-print will work. When at a loss, simply put on a black dress with a houndstooth scarf and smile. You may be on University Boulevard, but you've already made it to heaven.

> ## "If you want to walk the heavenly streets of gold, you gotta know the password, 'Roll, Tide, Roll.'"
> — Bear Bryant

Location: Tuscaloosa, AL

Division: West

Stadium: Bryant-Denny

Capacity: 101,821

Mascot: Crimson Tide

Mascot Name: Big Al (an elephant)

Colors: Crimson and White

Band: Million Dollar Band
("Even our band has its own video." - Joe Whitt, III, Alabama Law Student)

Rivals: Auburn, LSU, Tennessee

SEC Championships: 1933, 1934, 1937, 1945, 1953, 1965, 1966, 1971, 1972, 1973, 1974, 1975, 1977, 1978, 1979, 1981, 1989, 1992, 1999, 2009

National Championships: 1925, 1926, 1930, 1934, 1941, 1961, 1964, 1965, 1973, 1978, 1979, 1992, 2009

Heisman Trophy Winners: Mark Ingram (2009)

"The definition of an atheist in Alabama is someone who doesn't believe in Bear Bryant."

- Wally Butts

Cheers to Know

At Kick off: "Roll! Tide! Roll!"

During the Game: "Sweet Home Alabama"
(Listen closely so you know the right time to chime in with "Roll, Tide, Roll.")

After a Win: "Rammer Jammer Yellow Hammer" is sung with vigor to
celebrate an Alabama victory:

Hey Tigers (insert opposing mascot here)

Hey Tigers

We just beat the hell outta you!

Rammer Jammer Yellow Hammer

Give'em hell Alabama

Most Commonly Heard Phrases:

"Roll Tide, baby. Roll Tide." "The Bear would be proud."

What is your favorite tradition about Alabama football?

"Winning." - Susan Truss, Alabama Law student

Alabama Tailgating
Must-haves

Dreamland BBQ
Houndstooth tablecloths
Change of game day clothes hanging from the tent
Shakers

Where to Tailgate

Quad: The Quad is in the middle of campus and is just a few sorority houses away from the stadium. It's also conveniently located close to The Strip, which is where you'll end up for post-game festivities. Certain Quad lots are for sale for a premium, and you cannot be guaranteed the same location every week. However, on the grassier part of The Quad, you don't have to pay; you just have to lug your own supplies, and the satellite hook ups, though fewer and farther in between, are certainly not impossible to find. Any spot on The Quad is a spot worth having.

Hot Spot

President's Mansion: If you can snag an invite to the President's Mansion before kickoff, do not turn it down! Put on your finest Belle attire, and enjoy rubbing elbows with people who donate buildings to the university.

The Strip: For your fix of drunken coeds and a trip down college lane, The Strip offers famous watering holes, pre-game lunch spots, and post-celebration flu remedies. You've struck game day gold if you can land a patio table at Phil's before kickoff. And the famous Galettes is within stumbling distance from the stadium; without a sign, you'll just have to feel it to know your close. For the full Alabama experience, start early in the week and keep close to The Strip. You don't want to miss these Tide staples:

Houndstooth
Phil's (Buffalo Phil's)
Bear Trap
Galettes

The Colonnade: If you can get a room here, you're set for all of your game day needs. Located a few first downs from the stadium and offering comfortable chic lodging for your football weekend, the Colonnade is for fans who prefer four-poster beds to mobile mansions.

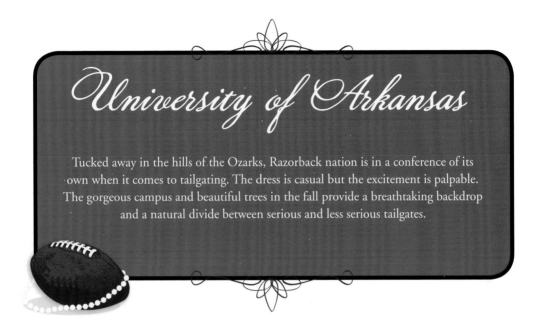

University of Arkansas

Tucked away in the hills of the Ozarks, Razorback nation is in a conference of its own when it comes to tailgating. The dress is casual but the excitement is palpable. The gorgeous campus and beautiful trees in the fall provide a breathtaking backdrop and a natural divide between serious and less serious tailgates.

Because of the vast and hill filled campus, you'll need the Arkansas game day staple of tennis shoes in order to tailgate-hop. Put your wardrobe worries away; as long as you're dressed in jeans and flannel and calling a pig (the mascot, Belles), you'll fit right in! Comfort is encouraged and practicality trumps couture at Razorback Stadium.

Arkansas faithful are just that: faithful, hospitable, and football enthusiasts. Of all of the stadiums and experiences, Arkansas is perhaps the most laidback in terms of party and fashion style, but hog fans' dedication to their team is not to be taken lightly. Thanks to their partly open stadium, fans can tailgate and watch players warm up at the same time. This is, by far, the most brilliant thing I've seen at any stadium.

You won't find many candelabras, strands of pearls, or high heels. You won't lose your hearing from the uproars of the crowd every weekend (unless they are playing Alabama, Auburn, or LSU). But you will find 72,000 wonderful people who gather in a beautiful pocket of the country where they call, roast, and support the Hogs. And that, Belles, is something remarkable in itself.

Location: Fayetteville, AR

Division: West

Stadium: Donald W. Reynolds Razorback Stadium

Capacity: 72,000

Stadium II: War Memorial Stadium in Little Rock, Arkansas

Capacity: 53,727

Mascot: Razorbacks

Mascot Name: Tusk

Colors: Cardinal-red and white

Band: The Razorback Marching Band

Rivals: Alabama, LSU

SEC Championships: None yet

National Championship: 1964

Heisman Trophy Winners: None yet

Battle Cry: "Wooooo, pig, sooie"

Cheers to Know

Kickoff: "Wooooo, pig, soooie!"

Full Hog Call: A full hog call is heard after a win. Motions are strongly encouraged.

Wooooo. Pig. Sooie!

Wooooo. Pig. Sooie!

Wooooo. Pig. Sooie!

Razorbacks!

Fight Song:

Arkansas Fight

Hit that line! Hit that line! Keep on going!Take that ball right down the field!Give a cheer. Rah! Rah!Never fear. Rah! Rah!Arkansas will never yield!On your toes, Razorbacks, to the finish,Carry on with all your might!For it's A-A-A-R-K-A-N-S-A-Sfor Arkansas!Fight! Fight! Fi-i-i-ight!

Things to Note:

Calling the Hogs: "Wooooo, pig, sooie!" There is precise form and technique to calling the hogs. It takes a little practice, but follow the leader. Raise your arms (with spirit fingers) high above you on the word "Woooo," pulling your arms down while crouching into a squat, and then straighten your arms back into the air on the word "Soooie." Players will be scoring touchdowns and pigs running your way in no time.

Arkansas Tailgating Must-haves

Bloody Marys
Flannel
BBQ
Rick's Bakery

Where to Tailgate

The Pit: Thanks to an open north end zone, The Pit combines a true fan's two favorite game day activities: grazing on tailgating spreads and watching pre-game warm-ups—my favorite part of Arkansas football! You'll even find devoted fans and Arkansas legends, such as Barry Switzer, acting as humble as your next-door neighbor.

Fraternity Row: The Greeks embrace game day with coed band parties on the front lawn and BBQ before kickoff. If you need to stumble to or from the game, you're in luck; the fraternity houses are a Hail Mary away from the stadium.

War Memorial Golf Course: Arkansas plays a handful of games in the state capital, hearkening back to the old days of college football. War Memorial Stadium is surrounded by an eighteen-hole golf course that serves more as a beautiful backdrop and landmark than a tailgating activity. Thanks to Little Rock's proximity to the lower half of the state, a fresh crowd of Razorback fans are always in attendance, making for an intense experience. Take note: fresh fans and a smaller stadium equal one lively day of calling the Hogs.

Hot Spot

Dickson Street: This is more of an after-game spot than a pre-game spot. In fact, it's eerily quiet before kickoff, but it is hardly maneuverable after a win.

Auburn University

In true Southern fashion, Auburn thrives on slow and steady. Whether they're tailgating, walking, cheering in the stadium, celebrating a win, shopping at J&M bookstore, or sipping freshly-squeezed lemonade at Toomer's Corner, the Auburn faithful prefer game day on The Plains at a refined pace.

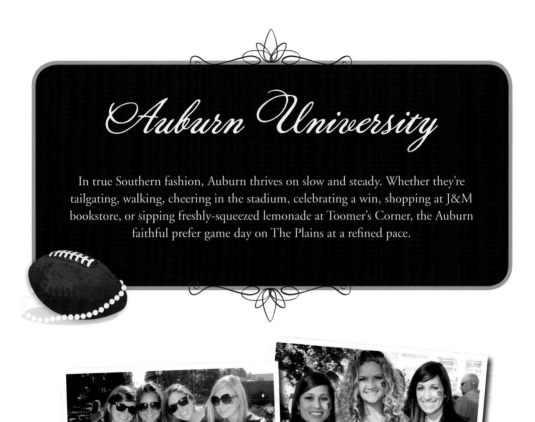

Tailgates are energized but not rambunctious. During the game, the fans are loud, but not deafening. Such characteristics lend themselves to impeccable stamina, allowing passionate celebrations, such as toilet-papering the trees on Toomer's Corner and firing up the grill for post-game tailgating. If you're visiting The Plains for the first time, get a good night's rest the day before; you'll be having a full day of fun.

What is a Belle to wear when visiting Auburn? Think understated elegance: tailored pants, well-fitted dresses, and the perfect amount of makeup. Auburn Belles have a classic style. If you are a Belle who takes the jersey route, the Auburn Belles pair jerseys with leggings, pearls, and sunglasses, making sure that their put-together look is only slightly less important than representing their favorite player.

Auburn, Alabama, may be the only place on Earth where walking around a tailgate with toilet paper stuck to your shoe is a source of pride rather than embarrassment! Be sure to pack extra two-ply in your touchdown purse when attending a game on The Plains. That cumbersome roll will be worth all the trouble when you launch it in Toomer's Corner after an Auburn win. If you forget to bring some TP from home, there are vendors nearby that sell extra-soft in bulk. Or, you can usually borrow some from the stadium; I'm pretty sure the cost is included in your ticket price!

Location: Auburn, AL

Division: West

Stadium: Jordan-Hare Stadium at Pat Dye Field

Capacity: 87,451

Mascot: Tigers

Mascot Name: Aubie

Colors: Navy and orange

Band: Auburn University Marching Band

Rivals: Alabama, Georgia, LSU

SEC Championships: 1957, 1983, 1987, 1988, 1989, 2004, 2010

National Championship: 1957, 2010

Heisman Trophy Winners: Pat Sullivan, 1975; Bo Jackson, 1981; Cameron Newton, 2010

Battle Cry: War (Damn) Eagle

"You can't go to heaven in a red canoe,
'cause God's favorite colors are orange and blue!"

Cheers to Know

Kickoff: "Waaaaaarrrrr Eagle, hey!"

Sung after an extra point: "Glory, glory to old Auburn; Glory, glory to old Auburn; glory, glory to old Auburn, A-U-B-U-R-N!"

Good ol' fashioned, crowd-rousing cheers:
"*I said it's great to be an Auburn Tiger*" (Most schools have tried to adopt the, "I said it's great to be" phrase, but it sounds best when wearing navy and orange.)

"*Bodygetta Bodygetta Bodygetta Bah Rah Rah Rah Sis Boom Bah Weagle Weagle War Damn Eagle Kick'em in the butt, Big Blue Hey!*"

Fight Song: War Eagle
War Eagle, fly down the field
Ever to conquer, never to yield
War Eagle, fearless and true,
Fight on you orange and blue
Go! Go! Go!
On to vict'ry, strike up the band
Give 'em hell, give 'em hell,
Stand up and yell, Hey!
War Eagle, win for Auburn,
Power of Dixie Land!

Most Notable:

Plastering (rolling) Toomers Corner with toilet paper after a win.

Eagle flying over the field before kickoff.

*Auburn Tailgating
Must-haves*

Toilet paper for rolling Toomers Corner
Sundresses
Monogrammed koozies

Where to Tailgate

The beautiful Plains of Auburn allow for tailgating in all corners of campus,
so festivities never feel too crowded or congested. However, to visit more than two tailgates
and make it to a 3:30 kickoff, you'll really need to boogie across campus.

The Green: A spacious grassy knoll between the Student Center and the Stadium that's
perfect for tailgating. Two Auburn alumni run a company called "Tailgate Guys" that provides tents,
equipment food, and all of your other tailgating needs. If you're in from out-of-town or want to
take a weekend off from doing all of the work, these guys are waiting for your call. Of course, you
are still strongly encouraged to supplement their set-up with your own personal Belle flare!

Grass: The hills and greenery on Auburn's campus provide an ideal backdrop for tailgating. Basically, if there is grass, you can set up your tailgate. Just be sure to include school buildings, street signs and other landmarks when telling your friends where to find you!

Amphitheater: If you're looking for a rowdy crowd among The Plains, look no further. For every home game in the fall, the amphitheater is crowded with a mix of students and recent alumni, who love to throw a heck of a football party, including loud music and an abundance of adult beverages. The people-watching alone is worth the trip.

Hot Spot

Big Blue Bagel: A quaint bagel shop where coeds, alumni, and fans flock early on game day... while curing the Friday-night flu. The casual, yet spirited, ambiance encourages even the faintest-of-heart to carb up before a long day of rapture on The Plains.

Toomer's Corner: An old pharmacy and Auburn landmark, Toomer's Corner sells university treasures and the most memorable, fresh-squeezed lemonade. Toomer's Corner is owned by the sweetest Tiger fan in the land, Betty Hoister. This is a must-see in the SEC.

The Vault: Conveniently located at the corner of University and Magnolia, the Vault is a high-ceiling bar with a large outdoor patio where live bands play. All generations gather here to have a good time before and after the games. The most commonly found items at the Vault are inebriated fans, wedding rings, and confiscated stadium cups, stacked high outside by the bouncer.

War Eagle:

Why does saying "War Eagle" turn two strangers into instant bosom buddies? Because "War Eagle" is the unifying Auburn battle cry. It's how students greet each other on campus; it's how two fans communicate while passing in a public place; it's how broken-hearted fans commiserate. The War Eagle legend has several variations, the common legend originated years ago when a Civil War veteran spotted an eagle circling the stadium during a close game between archrivals Auburn and Georgia. Immediately after the Auburn victory, the eagle fell to its death in the middle of the field. This eagle was called a War Eagle and has been a symbol of the dedication of the Auburn community ever since. Watching the eagle soar above the stadium minutes before kickoff is one of the most magical moments in all of college football.

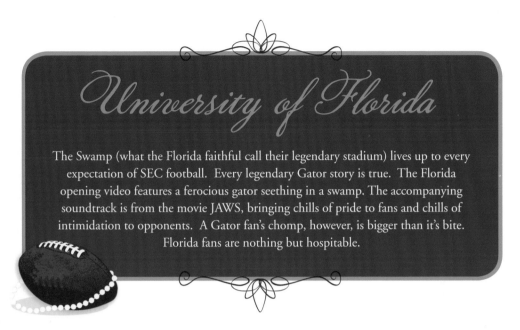

University of Florida

The Swamp (what the Florida faithful call their legendary stadium) lives up to every expectation of SEC football. Every legendary Gator story is true. The Florida opening video features a ferocious gator seething in a swamp. The accompanying soundtrack is from the movie JAWS, bringing chills of pride to fans and chills of intimidation to opponents. A Gator fan's chomp, however, is bigger than it's bite. Florida fans are nothing but hospitable.

Graced with vibrant blue and orange school colors, Florida Belles can adorn themselves in everything from shorts and a blue T-shirt, to an orange dress with blue jewels. There's even a trend of carrying Vera Bradley backpacks or monogrammed bags for easy access to lip gloss, cameras, and a drink of choice. The fashion norm is anything blue and orange, whether it's original or NCAA-trademarked. Some Belles even make dresses out of XL T-shirts or Tebow jerseys. Florida Belles can pull off just about anything with their charm, hospitality, and beauty.

Never fear finding a parking spot near the stadium; countless college students sell parking spaces behind their houses off of University Avenue, which is located a short walk to the stadium and gameday festivities. You'll feel the spirit of the crowd before you know them. Florida fans are generous, dedicated and always ready to share their traditions with you. When in company with Gator fans, you're in company with some of the SEC's finest.

Location: Gainesville, FL

Division: East

Stadium: Ben Hill Griffin Stadium at Florida Field

Nickname: The Swamp

Capacity: 88,548

Mascot: Gators

Mascot Names: Albert and Alberta, seriously dating, but not yet married.

Colors: Orange and Blue

Band: The Pride of the Sunshine

Rivals: Georgia, South Carolina (because of Coach Spurrier), Tennessee

SEC Championships: 1984, 1991, 1993, 1994, 1995, 1996, 2000, 2006, 2008

National Championships: 1996, 2006, 2008

Heisman Trophy Winners: Steve Spurrier (1966), Danny Wuerful (1996), Tim Tebow (2008)

"If you ain't a gator, you must be gator-bait."

Most notable for

The Gator Chomp

Florida fans all over the country will use both arms as Gator jaws to show their pride and domination over another team. It is one of the most recognizable fan gestures in college football. Mocking chomps from an opposing fan or player tend to infuriate the Gator Nation after a Florida loss.

Tim Tebow

One of college football's greatest athletes of all time, an upstanding citizen and a phenomenal quarterback. Known for his jump pass, his ability to throw and run with equal effectiveness, and his innate leadership. Tim Tebow's #15 Denver Broncos jersey was the biggest seller of his NFL rookie season.

Two in One

University of Florida is the first school to ever hold the Division I men's basketball title and the BCS football title in the same year: 2006.

Cheers to Know

Kick-off: There is not a cheer with words for kick-off; rather, fans start a slow Gator Chomp, which gets progressively faster as kick-off approaches. Usually the crowd makes some kind of "whoosh" sound once the ball is kicked.

Go Gators!: Introduced by a rapidly increasing Gator Chomp and a cue from the band. Often used to celebrate a first-down or impressive tackle.
"Go Gators! Go Gators! Go Gators! Come on Gators, get up and go!"

"We are the Boys from Old Florida": In between the third and fourth quarters Gator fans lock arms and sway as they sing:

We are the boys from old Florida
F - L - O - R - I - D - A
Where the girls are the fairest,
the boys are the squarest
of any old state down our way. (Hey!)
We are all strong for old Florida,
down where the old Gators play. (Go Gators!)
In all kinds of weather,
we'll all stick together, for
F - L - O - R - I - D - A

Florida Tailgating Must-Haves

Painkiller Drink from Bull Gator lot
Publix Fried Chicken
Pimento Cheese

Where to Tailgate

Bull Gator Lot: This is where the big-dollar donors rub elbows.
These fans forgo wearing the notorious Florida "jorts" (jean shorts)and enjoy
a very short walk to their fancy stadium entrance.

University Avenue: Directly across the street from the stadium is University Avenue,
which can teach you more about SEC fandom than any university. Here you'll find thousands
of fans, temporary team shops, tailgating tents, and fratty bars such as The Swamp (my all-time
favorite bar in the SEC), Balls, and Salty Dog.

Fraternity Row: Get ready for Fraternity and Sorority stars pre-gaming and showing-off
gameday outfits. A great place for free beer and entertaining shenanigans.

Hot Spot

The Swamp Bar: If you want to catch the other games of the day before heading into The Swamp (the stadium), head to The Swamp (the bar), where you'll find two stories of flat screens and an outdoor patio. Locals, fans, students and observers come together at this bar to partake in their pre-game rituals in the sunshine state.

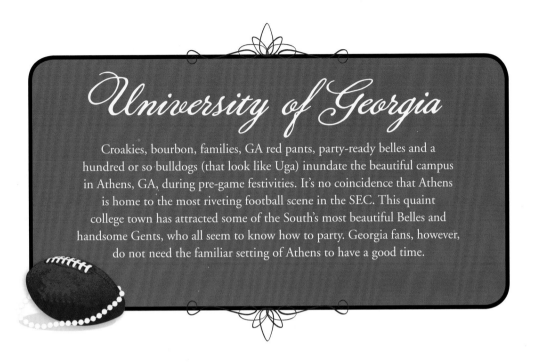

University of Georgia

Croakies, bourbon, families, GA red pants, party-ready belles and a hundred or so bulldogs (that look like Uga) inundate the beautiful campus in Athens, GA, during pre-game festivities. It's no coincidence that Athens is home to the most riveting football scene in the SEC. This quaint college town has attracted some of the South's most beautiful Belles and handsome Gents, who all seem to know how to party. Georgia fans, however, do not need the familiar setting of Athens to have a good time.

Never taking a week off, people of the Red-and-Black dress tailgate and celebrate away games with the same fanaticism that they show for home games. If you can't make it to Athens to see the sights, stay put, DAWG fans will bring the Georgia tailgating party to you.

The sound of the victory bell is music to your ears, but you'll regret being late to the game if you don't arrive in time to hear the lone trumpeter playing the opening lines of the "Battle Hymn of the Republic." There are few things more patriotic than a fall day in the heart of one of America's favorite college towns.

Location: Athens, GA

Division: East

Stadium: Sanford Stadium at Sanford Field

Nickname: Playing between the hedges

Capacity: 92,746

Mascot: Bulldogs (more commonly referred to as DAWGS)

Mascot Name: Uga VIII

Colors: Red and Black

Band: University of Georgia Red Coat Marching Band

Rivals: Florida, Auburn, Kentucky

SEC Championships: 1942, 1946, 1948, 1959, 1966, 1968, 1976, 1980, 1981, 1982, 2002, 2005

National Championships: 1942, 1980

Heisman Trophy Winners: Frank Sinkwich (1942), Herschel Walker (1982)

Most notable for

Herschel Walker: Renowned as the greatest player to ever wear a Georgia jersey, Herschel Walker was a Heisman Trophy finalist three times before winning the award in 1982. As a freshman, Walker was instrumental in Georgia's national title win over Notre Dame in the Sugar Bowl. To many Georgia faithful, Herschel Walker is the equivalent of Alabama's Bear Bryant.

Playing Between the Hedges: Georgia started the trend of SEC fields being lined with shrubbery; these hedges contribute to the old-school, Southern feel of Athens.

The World's Largest Outdoor Cocktail Party: The annual Florida-Georgia game, held in neutral Jacksonville, FL, has earned national recognition as a must-do for any college football fan. Florida and Georgia fans descend on St. Simon or St. George's Island for a long weekend to celebrate the rivalry. Imagine combining two tradition-rich, drinking-prone, beach-loving groups of fans into one weekend. Add a football game, and you have the best party south of the Mason Dixon Line.

Cheers to Know

Bark: "GOOOOOO DAWGS! Sic' em! Woof Woof Woof Woof Woof…."

After Touch Downs:
Glory Glory to Ol' Georgia
Glory Glory to Ol' Georgia
Glory Glory to Ol' Georgia
To hell with Kentucky! (Insert opponent)

General Rousing Chant: "Who's that comin' down the track?"
Leader: Who's that comin' down the track?
Followers: Who's that comin' down the track
It's a mean machine in red and black! (Followers repeat)
Ain't nothin' finer in the land… (Followers repeat)
Than a drunk obnoxious Georgia fan! (Followers repeat)
GO DAWGS! (Followers repeat)
GO DAWGS! (Followers repeat)
Everyone: "GOOOOOOOOOOOOO DAWGS! Sic' em! Woof Woof Woof Woof Woof…"

Georgia Tailgating Must-Haves

Chick-Fil-A
Pretty Belles
A bulldog

Where to Tailgate

North Campus: Tucked between two beautiful buildings and behind manicured landscaping, North Campus is home to family-friendly tailgating. Alumni gather for homecomings; new couples host their first tailgates; and young Herschel Walker wannabes practice their catching. North Campus showcases the best of what DAWG fans have to offer!

Open Recruitment: There are countless tailgating spots in Athens; often staking out space is a free-for-all. Pitch a tent wherever you see a spot. A few notable areas are:

South Campus by Stegeman Coliseum (basketball arena)
Fraternity houses near Meyer Hall
Downtown Athens

You can't go wrong with a tailgate, as long as you're within the city limits of Athens!

University of Kentucky

Kentucky fans are known as some of the most passionate fans in the SEC. They have a rich tradition of battling the giants of the SEC with "house money," but the Big Blue Nation supports every Kentucky athletic team with vigor. Kentucky fans are loud. Kentucky fans are loyal, and upon my word, Kentucky fans will travel! Football may not be the strongest Wildcat sport, but Wildcat fans love their team to a fault. You'll be lured into the Big Blue Nation by the pretty Belles and abundance of bourbon; be warned, CATS fans will become absolutely irate over a bad call, an interception, or a Wildcat loss—all of which you will unavoidably hear about until basketball season.

Kentucky fans hail from all corners of the state, or as they say, "from Pikeville to Paducah" and "from Mayfield to Morehead." You'll inevitably hear a unique Southern drawl. When Kentuckians cheer for the CATS, they sound like they're cheering for the "CAYUTS" (pronounced "cay"-"yats") in their distinctive Kentucky dialect.

Nearby Keeneland racetrack is not for the casual fan. Spending a full day in heels and sipping good Kentucky bourbon is not for the faint of heart. The prestige of Keeneland contributes to the distinct, classy look of Bluegrass Belles with their meticulously applied makeup. It's not surprising to see Belles dressed up in Kentucky blue T-shirts and designer dresses at the same tailgate. All are welcome; all are diehards; all are there for the party.

Location: Lexington, KY

Division: East

Stadium: Commonwealth Stadium at C.M. Newton Field

Mascot: Wildcats

Mascot Name: Scratch

Colors: Kentucky Blue and White

Most commonly heard phrase: "Basketball starts in December"

Rivals: Georgia, Tennessee, Vanderbilt

Band: Wildcat Marching Band

SEC Championships: 1950, 1976

National Championships: See above comment about basketball

Heisman Trophy Winners: See above comment about basketball

Most notable for

Keeneland racetrack: It's only fitting that Kentucky football includes Kentucky thoroughbreds. Located a few miles from campus, Keeneland racetrack provides a beautiful setting for Belles and Gents alike to enjoy everything that epitomizes the Bluegrass State: fast horses, smooth bourbon, and pretty Belles. All fans throw gentility out the window to cheer wildly for their Wildcats on the gridiron. You'd be remiss if you made the trip to Lexington for a night game and didn't start the day off at the world-renowned racetrack.

Basketball: The Kentucky Wildcat basketball team has made fourteen Final Four appearances in the NCAA tournament and has won seven NCAA tournament championships. UK basketball is a force to be reckoned with. Unfortunately, Rupp Arena is not conducive to tailgating!

Cheers to Know

CATS: This cheer is used throughout the game and is often not instigated by the cheerleaders. Heard wherever more than one Kentucky fan is present, your visceral reaction to the blue and white harmony will have you cheering for the CATS even if you're at a bar! "C-A-T-S, CATS, CATS, CATS!"

Fight Song:
"On, On U of K"
We are right for the fight today!
Hold that ball and hit that line;
Every Wildcat star will shine.
We'll fight, fight, fight
For the blue and white,
As we roll to that goal, Varsity
And we'll kick, pass and run
'Til the battle is won,
And we'll bring home the victory!
"My Old Kentucky Home"

My Old Kentucky Home is played before and after a game and is treated with as much, perhaps more, reverence as the National Anthem.

Kentucky Tailgating Must-Haves

Beer cheese
Motorized coolers
Bourbon

Where to Tailgate

Red or Blue Lot: Creating a sea of Kentucky blue tents and clouds of smoke
from busy grills, the massive parking lot surrounding Commonwealth Stadium makes
it clear to all visitors that Kentucky fans are serious about tailgating. These lots are
usually filled with older fans with parking passes and cash flow. This is the perfect
venue for bringing your family, your fellow alumni, and out-of-towners to see just
how dedicated Wildcat fans are. Be prepared to taste homemade beer cheese dip
and wash it down with full-bodied KY bourbon or Ale-8.

Johnson Center Fields: Southern hospitality is not lacking at the fraternity tailgates
behind the Johnson Center fields. You'll find beautiful coeds and recent alumni celebrating
everything college (and post-college) has to offer: thousands of friends, copious amounts of

bourbon, and hopeful conversations about the impending game that encourage you to forget responsibilities. Multiple fraternities team up for big games, pooling their money to bring in well-known bands. In the Bluegrass State, hosting before and after a game is a Gent's specialty, and Belles in blue are always welcome.

Hot Spots

Ramsey's: A perfect cure for the Friday night flu, the colossal Southern-style breakfast at Ramsey's will feed your entire pledge class. Popular among college students and people of all ages for the happy hours and perfect Bloody Marys and LITs.

Downtown Lexington: Downtown is an up-and-coming area to celebrate pre- and post-games. It's safe, clean, pretty and packed with bars, which include Cheapside, Bluegrass Tavern, Wildcat Saloon, and SkyBar. Nearby, Redmon's offers a Southern dive bar experience. If North Campus is too crowded and you've already eaten at Tally-Ho, head downtown and take in the scene.

Two Keys: Two Keys is *the* college bar in Lexington. It's plastered with UK memorabilia, banners, and autographs. A mammoth patio beckons with its charm. Not a game day goes by without a Big Blue crowd. Two Keys is the third leg of the Lexington "Triple Crown" – starting your day at Keeneland, going to the football game, then closing down Two Keys. If you can party that long, Two Keys is a must!

Louisiana State University

The pride that hovers over the state of Louisiana is second to none; experiencing game day in Baton Rouge epitomizes the heart and glory of SEC football. LSU fans are among the most spirited, dedicated and fun-loving you'll ever meet. Some use the term "obnoxious," to describe LSU faithfuls, but it's really just hyper-fandom. Their cheers are deafening, electric, and earth-shattering. Whether LSU fans say their prayers en Francais or in Cajun, they have certainly been answered with a prestigious football program.

Be warned. LSU fans will, on occasion, vehemently yell at you over a bad play, and then turn around and offer you a bowl of jambalaya with potato salad and a fresh Albita™ beer. If you're from the opposing team, you will inevitably be taunted with the famous "Tiger Bait;" no man, woman, or child is spared from heckling if they aren't wearing purple and gold.

It's against Cajun law in Baton Rouge to turn down an invitation to be with friends and fans for a good time. Hospitality and delicious food are simply part of Tiger fans' DNA. Coming hungry to tailgates is a must. You'll be offered Cajun delicacies such as pastalaya, alligator sauce piquante, and crawfish étouffée (your pallet will never forget Baton Rouge).

Are LSU Belles the same as the rest? Goodness no! LSU Belles are a little more casual, a little more rambunctious, a little more involved, a little more excitable. They wear a wardrobe that matches: any sort of tiger print, all shades of purple and gold, and the all-business jeans and LSU T-shirt. You'll never be underdressed or overdressed in Tiger Stadium as long as you're covered head to toe in spirit.

If you are in search of a perpetual Southern celebration, hungry for Cajun cuisine, or enjoy turning strangers into friends, look no further. Death Valley is the heaven for you.

Location: Baton Rouge, LA

Division: West

Stadium: Tiger Stadium

Nickname: Death Valley

Capacity: 91,600

Mascot: Tigers

Mascot Name: Mike the Tiger

Colors: Purple and Gold

Band: Golden Band from Tigerland

> The Golden Girls, the danceline of LSU, are impossible to overlook and totally unforgettable.

Rivals: Anywhere Nick Saban is coaching, Alabama, Arkansas, Auburn, Ole Miss

SEC Championships: 1935, 1936, 1958, 1961, 1970, 1986, 1988, 2001, 2003, 2007

National Championships: 1958, 2003, 2007

Heisman Trophy Winners: Billy Cannon (1959)

"I'd rather face the lions in the Coliseum than the Tigers in Baton Rouge."

— Bobby Dodd

Cheers to Know

Kickoff: L-S-U!

Geaux Tigers: "Geaux Tigers!" Pronounced "Go." This is commonly played after extra points or whenever the Band Major thinks the team deserves some extra encouragement!

Tiger Bait: "Tiger bait. Tiger Bait." This is a taunt for the opposing-team fans. Be forewarned: opposing fans should fear spending time in Mike the Tiger's $7 million dollar cage if LSU loses at home.

Fight Song: Played throughout the game, mostly after touchdowns. This is the one you've been hearing your mama sing in the kitchen for years.

"Hey Fighting Tigers"
Hey, Fightin' Tigers, Fight all the way.
Hey, Fightin' Tigers, win the game today.
You've got the know-how,
You're doing fine,
Hang on to the ball as you hit the wall
And smash right through the line.
You've got to go for the touchdown.
Run! Up the score!
Make Mike the Tiger stand right up and roar.
ROAR!
Give it all of your might as you fight tonight
and keep the goal in view.
Victory for L-S-U!

Most notable for

"Quake of '88": In the last two minutes of the LSU-Auburn game of 1988, LSU beat Auburn 7-6 in Tiger Stadium. The eruption of cheers from the full stadium tipped off the seismograph in an LSU science lab. Scientists all over the country were shocked by the unseasonable and unpredicted earthquake. Turns out, it was just an SEC football game in Tiger Stadium.

Tiger Stadium: Known as one of the loudest stadiums in the country, hence its nickname, "Deaf Stadium." LSU fans are more than capable of causing turnovers and penalties with their noise.

Les Miles: Coach Miles is notorious for pulling off last-minute trick plays, nearly giving LSU fans heart attacks followed by adulation.

Chinese Bandits: The LSU band plays the Chinese Bandits tune whenever LSU's defense forces a turnover. A stunning way to give due credit to a hard-working defense.

Louisiana State Tailgating Must-Haves

Cajun Food: (Cook Me Somethin' Mister! Jambalaya)
A plethora of adult beverages
Loud party speakers for music

Where to Tailgate

Parade Grounds: You'll need your "tape and tent" combo. Set up the night before and get an early start on game day to take in the full experience. Fraternities often have multiple tents, and pledges usually deliver couches and kegs. Although it's a bit of a hike to the stadium, Parade Grounds provides plenty of open space for every sort of LSU pre-game ritual and celebration.

RV Lot: RVs at LSU are among the finest in the country. With rows of mobile mansions filling the lot, loyal fans and visitors have access to some of the best food in the region, the cleanest bathrooms in Baton Rouge, and the coldest air conditioning before an early-season game. The massive RV family at LSU is second to none, propelling the Tiger game day experience to one you'll never forget.

Indian Mounds: Two large mounds that are thousands of years old and traditionally serve as a slide and gridiron for young tailgaters. Families and serious tailgaters have used the Mounds as their backdrops and landmarks for generations. Nowadays, they party at the base of the Mounds due to the university's initiative to preserve them.

Hot Spots

Walk Ons, Chimes or anywhere else in Tigerland: Bars that welcome everybody looking for a Louisiana Saturday night.

Post Game Tailgating: You can go out to the bars, but the party is already at your tailgate. LSU is notorious for keeping the party going after a game, win or lose.

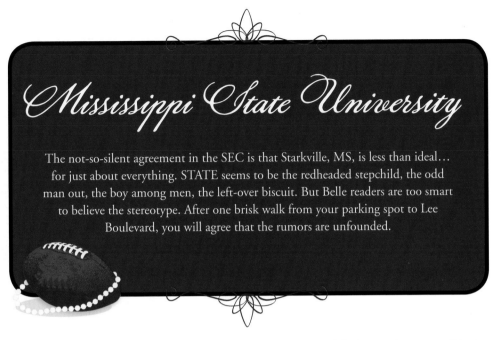

Mississippi State University

The not-so-silent agreement in the SEC is that Starkville, MS, is less than ideal…
for just about everything. STATE seems to be the redheaded stepchild, the odd
man out, the boy among men, the left-over biscuit. But Belle readers are too smart
to believe the stereotype. After one brisk walk from your parking spot to Lee
Boulevard, you will agree that the rumors are unfounded.

There are two options for your Saturday activities in Starkville: fully immersing yourself in the
gridiron commotion or going out of town. Outside of Lee Boulevard and The Junction, you'll
find a ghost town atmosphere that rivals any in the SEC.

Starkville tailgating is precisely organized, immaculately cleaned, and systemically lined with
maroon tents. Do not mistake their organization for stiffness. STATE fans have a big ole time,
all the while offering strangers tickets, dinner, and a chance to see what STATE fans call, "the
real Mississippi school."

Don't bother to pull out your shiny shoes or fancy dresses for a game in Starkville. Bulldog Belles are more casual when showing their spirit. They often pair a maroon shirt with a skirt, wear a cotton dress, or don a simple T-shirt and jeans. Before you attend a STATE game, be sure to see what the coach has requested. Davis Wade stadium is rather quaint: capacity is 55,082, but 54,999 fans will show their spirit by wearing all white when the coach designates "white out" game. Quaint or not, the heart of Mississippi resides in Starkville.

Location: Starkville, MS

Division: West

Stadium: Davis Wade Stadium at Scott Field

Capacity: 55,082

Mascot: Bulldogs

Mascot name: Bully

Colors: Maroon and White

Band: The Famous Maroon Band

Rivals: Ole Miss

SEC Championships: None yet

National Championship: None yet

Heisman Trophy Winners: None yet

Most notable for

Cowbells: Legend has it that many moons ago, a cow walked onto the field at Mississippi State during a victorious game over archrival Ole Miss. Cowbells have been a fixture at STATE ever since, despite the ban that the NCAA placed on noisemakers. You'd be hard-pressed to spend a game day in Starkville without appreciating the variations of cowbells that Bulldog supporters have engineered.

Egg Bowl: The Egg Bowl is the annual rival game played between Mississippi State and "that school up North," Ole Miss. The name refers to the egg-shaped footballs of 1927, when an official trophy was presented to the winning team. The rivalry alternates between Starkville and Oxford, Mississippi, and is always the most important game of the season.

Cheers to Know

After a touchdown: "Go! State! Go State!"

When playing Ole Miss: "Hotty Toddy, gosh Almighty, when's Ole Miss going to be somebody?"

Fight Song: "Hail State"
Hail dear 'ole State!
Fight for that victory today.
Hit that line and tote that ball,
Cross the goal before you fall!
And then we'll yell, yell, yell, yell!
For dear 'ole State we'll yell like H-E-L-L!
Fight for Mis-sis-sip-pi State,
Win that game today!

Mississippi State Tailgating Must-Haves

Dog Bone Sugar Cookies
BBQ
Cowbells

Where to Tailgate

The Junction: The Junction is comprised of hundreds of acres of beautiful grass beneath endless rows of maroon and white tents on game day. You may become overwhelmed by the sheer number of tents, but follow the straight lines painted on the grass, and you'll eventually find a nice STATE fan willing to direct you to your destination. Located off Lee Boulevard, directly in front of Denis Wade Stadium, The Junction is the most conveniently located tailgating spot in the SEC.

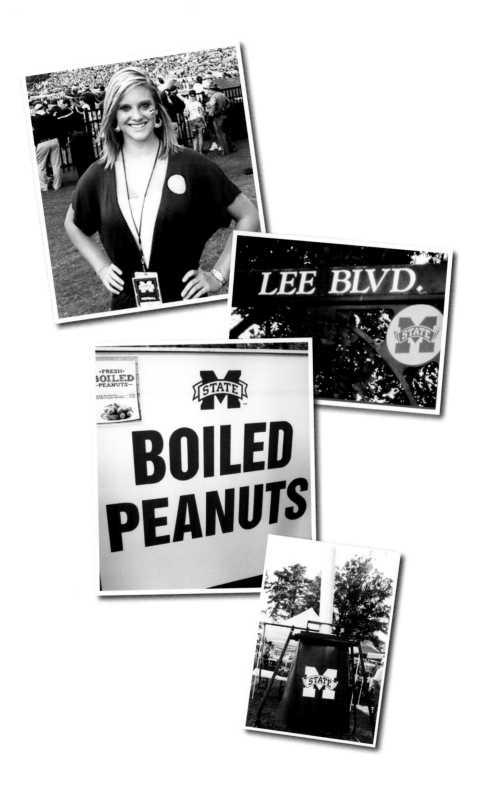

University of Mississippi

The South will never rise again, but in Oxford, Mississippi, part of it never truly fell. Silver is given no time to tarnish, propriety is still held in high regard (even when over-served), and Gents, luckily for us Belles, still act like men of genteel upbringings.

If the Antebellum style of each columned building (including sorority and fraternity houses) doesn't make you feel a part of Dixie, taking a leisurely walk down "O'Hara Lane" or through the neighborhoods of "Tara Road" and "Twelve Oaks" certainly will. But you don't need to know much about *Gone With the Wind* to recognize that the same amount of pride is found in Oxford as was in Scarlett.

What's not to be proud of? The Grove single-handedly raises the bar for tailgating at every other SEC school. Such a prestigious reputation comes from strict adherence to unspoken, yet strictly enforced, rules.

Take the dress code, for example. Although Ole Miss colors are not required, nothing less than your Sunday best is acceptable (assuming your Sunday best belongs on a runway). Designer everything is preferred, from your sunglasses to your high heels.

When tailgating, candelabras, floral arrangements, McCarty pottery, tablecloths, flat-screen TVs, and polished silver are not to be forgotten. Doing so would drop your tailgate to the caliber of "other SEC schools," and that is frowned upon at Ole Miss.

Be knowledgeable about the coaches and the Rebel gridiron heroes. But if you've worked hard to pull off a high-quality tailgate, do not feel obligated to go into the stadium. Sit a spell and enjoy watching the other games on TV.

Few words can capture the true essence of ecstasy that home-game weekends inspire. Cares are forgotten. The outside world disappears. All of life stands still. Oxford is God's personal choice for Saturdays in Dixie.

Location: Oxford, Mississippi

Division: West

Stadium: Vaught-Hemingway Stadium at Hollingsworth Field

Capacity: 60,580

Mascot: Rebels

On-field Mascot: Black Bear (Come find me at a tailgate, and I'll explain this one. It's at least a one-drink explanation!)

Mascot Name: Rebel Black Bear

Colors: Navy, Red, and White

Band: The Pride of the South

Rivals: Mississippi State, LSU, Vanderbilt

SEC Championships: 1947, 1954, 1955, 1960, 1962, 1963

National Championships: 1959, 1960, 1962

Heisman Trophy Winners: None yet

"We may have lost a game or two, but we've never lost a tailgate."

Cheers to Know

"Hotty Toddy"
Are you ready? Hell yeah, damn right!
Hotty Toddy! Gosh almighty! Who the hell are we?
Hey! Flim Flam! Bim Bam!
Ole Miss, by damn!

Fight Song:
"Forward Rebels"
Forward, Rebels, march to fame,
Hit that line and win this game
We know that you'll fight it through,
For your colors, red and blue.
Rah, rah, rah!
Rebels, you are the Southland's pride,
Take that ball and hit your stride,
Don't stop 'til the victory's won
for your Ole Miss.
Fight, fight for your Ole Miss!

Ole Miss Tailgating Must-Haves

Dog Bone Sugar Cookies
BBQ
Cowbells

Where to Tailgate

The Grove: This is the only acceptable place to tailgate in Oxford. Look for acres of tents, droves of beautiful coeds, seersucker and sundresses, and wedding-sized buffets. Tailgating in the Grove is an art form. Going to an Ole Miss football game without tailgating in the Grove is like going to Disney World as a young Belle and not visiting Cinderella's castle. Just don't forget to set up the night before, and "put it (your drink) in a cup!"

Rebel Walk: If there is time after enjoying your five-star dining experience under a navy and red tent, the Rebel Walk is a must-see as players and coaches make their way to the stadium through The Grove.

Hot Spots

Hotty Toddy Potty: The most sophisticated port-a-pottys in the SEC are located strategically around The Grove.

The Square: A charming town built around Oxford's town hall. You'll find the South's oldest department store, Neilson's, selling chic game day outfits. Square Books sells books about Mississippi and hosts authors from all parts of Dixie. A plethora of restaurants and bars for pre-and-post game celebrations are here, as well as plenty of opportunities to people-watch for the novice game day attendee. Don't forget to stop by Big Bad Breakfast or City Grocery to really feel part of the Oxford community before kickoff.

University of South Carolina

South Carolina fans are among the most dedicated and fervent of the SEC, despite their late arrival to the conference in 1992. When attending a game in Columbia, South Carolina, you'll feel the passion of every fan even though most tailgaters eat their own mascot in the form of take-out from Bojangles (the chicken 'n biscuits restaurant). Even more impressive is the Gamecock presence at an SEC Championship game. The loyal black-and-garnet fans shout thunderous cheers for their gridiron heroes, persisting for four straight quarters.

Williams-Brice Stadium is surrounded by the South Carolina Fairgrounds, the state Farmer's Market, and continual construction of new condo buildings. Navigating your way to the stadium is an industrial haul that proves quite a challenge to voyage in heels. Your style, however, should not prohibit you from experiencing all of the tailgating spots that Columbia has to offer: The Fairgrounds, Carolina Park, Cocks' Corner, and 5 Points, to name a few. Wherever you are, be prepared: you're going to hear a lot of very beautiful Belles screaming, "Go Cocks!"

Some South Carolina Belles are interested in getting down to business in jerseys. Others pull out all the stops with long dresses, high heels, and perfectly coordinated touchdown purses. Gamecock Belles are festive, enthusiastic, and never stuffy. While the general Gamecock population tends to lean toward preppy game day gear, if you are heading to a game in Columbia, you have your choice of wardrobe, as long as it includes garnet and black.

Location: Columbia, South Carolina

Division: East

Stadium: Williams-Brice

Nickname: The Cockpit

Capacity: 80,250

Mascot: Gamecocks

Mascot Name: Cocky

Colors: Garnet and Black

Band: The Mighty Band of the Southeast

Rivals: Auburn, Florida, Georgia, Tennessee,

SEC Championships: None yet

National Championships: None yet

Heisman Trophy Winners: George Rogers (1980)

"God is smiling on the Gamecocks."

- Steve Spurrier

Cheers to Know

Kickoff: "Goooooooooooooooooo (ball is kicked) Cocks...Fight, Win, Kick A**!"

Crowd Rousers:
"U-S-C, Gooooo Cocks!"
"Gooo…."''"…Cocks"

Fight Song: "The Fighting Gamecocks Lead the Way"
Hey, let's give a cheer, Carolina is here,
The Fighting Gamecocks lead the way.
Who gives a care, if the going gets tough,
And when it is rough, that's when the 'Cocks get going.
Hail to our colors of garnet and black,
In Carolina pride have we.
So, go Gamecocks go - FIGHT!
Drive for the goal - FIGHT!
USC will win today - GO COCKS!
So, let's give a cheer, Carolina is here.
The Fighting Gamecocks All The Way!

Most Notable:

Visors: Every man, boy, and head-coach in Columbia has a lucky game day visor. Coach Spurrier started this trend and can often be glimpsed on the sideline, throwing his on the ground. Wherever you see Gamecock fans, you see Gamecock visors.

South Carolina Tailgating Must-Haves

Bojangles and Publix subs
Gamecock or Palmetto Koozie
Boiled Peanuts from Cromers, "Guaranteed Worst in Town"

Where to Tailgate

Cockaboose Railroad: With twenty-two cockabooses permanently parked outside of Williams-Brice, owners of these garnet railroad cars are able to host their tailgates with the convenience of cable, bathrooms, air-conditioning, and kitchenettes. Stop by to see how Gamecocks celebrate game day, it's a must see in the SEC!

Morrison Memorial Lot: A wonderful fenced-off, grassy area where young professionals and lifetime Greek enthusiasts tailgate. The focus here is on networking and boozing; you won't find elaborate tailgate spreads, but you'll find a full lot of attractive Gamecock fans showing their pride.

The Farmer's Market: This new area in front of Williams-Brice previously served as a giant farmer's market, but has now been transformed into a 3,000-spot parking lot with a grassy knoll, plush landscape, and a straight shot to the Cockpit.

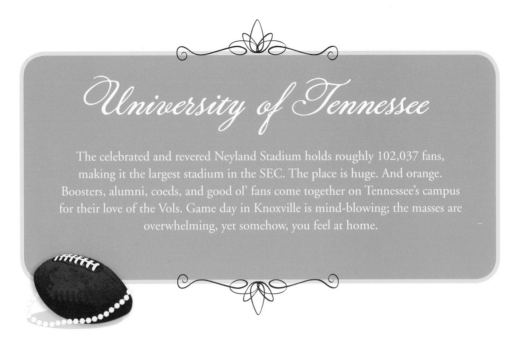

University of Tennessee

The celebrated and revered Neyland Stadium holds roughly 102,037 fans, making it the largest stadium in the SEC. The place is huge. And orange. Boosters, alumni, coeds, and good ol' fans come together on Tennessee's campus for their love of the Vols. Game day in Knoxville is mind-blowing; the masses are overwhelming, yet somehow, you feel at home.

Tennessee is certainly an SEC contender for size, pride and the sheer number of fans who pack the sacred stadium. Every fan wears something orange. However, finding the perfect UT orange proves difficult, so many UT Belles simply purchase a pair of overalls and dip them in a bucket of orange paint!

Wherever your allegiance lies, thanks to the free spirit and hospitable personalities of Tennessee fans, it feels like homecoming every week. The Volunteer faithful are rowdy; they are passionate; but above all, they believe in all things orange. And unlike their end-zone, their pride is solid, not checkered.

"The game of football is beginning to gain foothold in Knoxville."

- Knoxville Journal, November 20, 1891

Location: Knoxville, Tennessee

Division: East

Stadium: Shields-Watkins Field at Neyland Stadium

Capacity: 102,459

Mascot: Volunteers

Mascot Name: Smokey (A Bluetick Coonhound)

Colors: Tennessee Orange and White

Band: Pride of the Southland

Rivals: Alabama, Florida, Kentucky, Vanderbilt,

SEC Championships: 1938, 1940, 1946, 1951, 1956, 1967, 1969, 1985, 1990, 1997, 1998

National Championship: 1938, 1940, 1950, 1951, 1967, 1998

Heisman Trophy Winners: None yet

"Tennessee sophomores don't deserve citizenship papers until they have survived a game against Alabama."

- General Neyland

Cheers to Know

Kickoff: "Ooooo, Let's go UT!"

Rocky Top: You'll hear "Rocky Top" in Neyland Stadium more times than you've heard your own name. If you can learn "Rocky Top" and sing it with vigor (time and time again), you'll be a true Tennessee fan in no time!

Rocky Top, you'll always be
Home sweet home to me
Good ol' Rocky Top, WHOO
Rocky Top Tennessee
Go Vols, Go! "V-O-L-S, V-O-L-S, V-O-L-S, go Vols go!"

Most Commonly Heard Phrase: Go Vols!

Most notable for

Vol Navy: One if by land, two if by sea, the Vol Navy is a must-see. Tennessee fans take full advantage of the Tennessee River's harbor by combining the joys of boating with the thrills of football. Floating tailgates add a unique flare to the SEC. Even if you don't have a friend with a boat, the "boatgaters" are famous for their hospitality to strangers. Whether or not you go aboard, head down to Volunteer Landing to take in this impressive sight.

Power T: You'll never find a larger assembly of orange than in Neyland Stadium. Top it off with orange-and-white-checkered end zones and the team entering through the Power T to the fight song, and you've got yourself an SEC tradition that will take your breath away every weekend.

The Rock: To know what's happening on Tennessee's campus, just take a stroll by the Rock. UT students show their sense of humor and artistic abilities by painting a gigantic rock with scenes that lampoon visiting teams. Stop by for a good laugh and a picture.

Tennessee Tailgating Must-Haves

Friend with a Yacht in the Vol Navy
Comfortable shoes for climbing the hills of Knoxville
Checkerboard Overalls

Where to Tailgate

G-10 Parking Deck: Acquiring a parking pass to the G-10 parking deck (just a short first down from the stadium) is as hard as going undefeated in the SEC. These tailgaters are festive, hospitable, and ever so orange. If you can't land a parking spot, just head over to G-10 and start making friends. With any luck, you'll have a spot for the next game.

Fiji Island: This island of grass in front of the fraternity houses provides plenty of space for all varieties of fans to tailgate, for the next generations of Vol players to practice, and for Belles to get some sun. This is one of my favorite areas for watching the Tennessee wardrobe trends and grabbing a bite to eat before heading to the stadium.

Vol Navy: Who doesn't love adding a cannonball competition to their tailgate? Albert Haynesworth, former UT defensive end, loves to tailgate on the docks and fly his Vol Navy flag from his multimillion dollar boat!

Hot Spots

The Strip (Cumberland Avenue): Home to Tin Roof (live music, beer pong), Tap Room (you must order the Cheese Bings), and countless other fratty establishments begging you to sing "Rocky Top" into the wee hours of the morning.

Old City: Old City is a quaint part of Knoxville that welcomes a slightly older crowd. If you're looking for some good food and a celebratory vibe, but want to avoid the crowd on The Strip, this is the place. Either way, warm up your vocal chords, because even off The Strip, you'll be singing "Rocky Top" into the wee hours of the morning!

Vanderbilt University

What is college football without overzealous fans who bypass a little thing called tailgating and don't enter the stadium before halftime? Think Vanderbilt.

What Vanderbilt fans lack in numbers (39,790 stadium capacity, 6,879 enrolled students) and winning seasons, they make up for in loyalty and academics. Vanderbilt fans are proud and protective of their football program (one of the oldest in the SEC) and continue to support their gridiron heroes with the same fervor as every other SEC team, just not always from within the stadium.

Vanderbilt's campus and stadium provides a relaxed environment, which serves as a welcomed change of pace during a full season of stadium-hopping. There is no need to feel rushed to clean up your tailgate or finish your biochemistry homework before kickoff; a majority of Vandy students rarely head into the stadium until the second quarter or second half, if at all. When Vandy fans finally do get to the game, you'll see well mannered fans stand to let others pass easily to their seats—which is commonly misinterpreted as a spirited version of the wave. Wave or no wave, fans with panache and courtesy is what the SEC is all about. And isn't that something to appreciate?

'Dores fans may have a general disregard for kickoff time, but they do not disregard their game day wardrobes. Vandy Belles are absolutely striking. Black and 14-karat gold are the universal attire. A dash of silver-spoon upbringing, a liberal amount of class, and a pinch of trust funds to maintain that chic designer look create the perfect recipe for Vandy Belles to look like, well, Vanderbilts, on game day.

And they are smart. Very smart. Sure, these Belles may focus more on being at the top of the class than on being the Belle of the tailgate, but what's not to love about a brilliant Southern woman? If they could just get into the stadium before halftime, we'd have some Belles of the SEC!

Location: Nashville, Tennessee

Division: East

Stadium: Vanderbilt Stadium at Dudley Field

Capacity: 39,790

Mascot: Commodores

Mascot Name: Mr. C

Colors: Black and Gold

Band: Spirit of Gold Band

Rivals: Kentucky, Ole Miss, Tennessee

SEC Championships: None yet

National Championship: Better to ask for National Academic rankings

Heisman Trophy Winners: Better to ask for Rhodes Scholars

Cheers to Know

Kick off: "Goooooooooo 'Dores!"

Crowd Rouser: "V-A-N-D-Y Vandy, Vandy, oh hell yes!"
"Who ya wit? V U!"

Fight Song: "Dynamite" is sung as the players take the
field and after they score a touchdown
Dynamite, dynamite,
When Vandy starts to fight.
Down the field with blood to yield
If need be save the shield.
If victory's won when battle's done,
Then Vandy's name will rise in fame.
Win or lose the fates will choose,
But Vandy's game will be the same.
Dynamite, dynamite,
When Vandy starts to fight!
V...A...N...D...Y...Vandy, Vandy, Go, Go, Go!

Most Commonly Heard Phrases:
"Are you going to the game?" is frequently asked during halftime in Vandyville.

"Basketball season is almost here. We'll get you then!"

Most Notable:

Football players' GPAs

Smart, beautiful girls

Showing up to the game late, not until the second half, or not at all

Vanderbilt Tailgating
Must-Haves

Barbeque from Whitt's or chicken from McDougal's
Academic discussion
A TV to watch all football games

Where to Tailgate

Vandyville: A row of tents on Natchez Trace that offers a central area
for tailgaters (consisting mostly of alumni and Nashville locals), and a view of
the portable Jumbotron as it broadcasts other SEC games.

Fraternity houses: A welcoming environment for undergrads or visiting coeds.
You're bound to have such a good time, you'll miss the first half of the game.

Holiday Inn Parking Lot: This is where the team's families tailgate. It's conveniently
located a few first downs away from the stadium, Vandyville, and the Vandy walk.

Hot Spots

Sam's Sports Bar: If you enjoy tailgating with Vandy fans, but want to catch the rest of the SEC games, Sam's in Hillsboro Village is the place to be. With good food and great coverage of games, Sam's is a close second to actually being at the game.

Tin Roof: A safe distance from the downtown tourist traps and located 2-3 miles from Vanderbilt's campus, the Tin Roof has live music every night. It's a hot spot for college kids and recent alumni. Just about any bar on Demonbreun Street or in The Gulch will give you a local fix.

The National Anthem

If we're going to highlight the South's greatest fight songs, we must not forget the greatest fight song of all time. On game day, opposing fans of rival teams prepare for battle, uniting to honor our country and the men and women who have so bravely served on our behalf. As Belles, we show respect by knowing every word. Keep your handkerchief nearby, the National Anthem is always a tear-jerker for me. And for goodness sakes, gentlemen, remove your hats!

The Star Spangled Banner
By Francis Scott Key (1814)

Oh, say can you see by the dawn's early light

What so proudly we hailed at the twilight's last gleaming

Whose broad stripes and bright stars thru the perilous fight,

O'er the ramparts we watched were so gallantly streaming

And the rocket's red glare, the bombs bursting in air,

Gave proof through the night that our flag was still there.

Oh, say does that star-spangled banner yet wave

O'er the land of the free and the home of the brave

Talking the Talk

Vocabulary

Backfield: Field behind the line of scrimmage (LOS). When players are referenced as being "in the backfield," it means they are not lined up on the line of scrimmage.

Blitz: A technique used by the defense when more defensive players cross the line of scrimmage than the offense has players to block them. There are corner blitzes and safety blitzes as well, and they all attempt to create pressure on the quarterback or to stop the run. Imagine: *All* your relatives blind-siding you with a surprise holiday visit.

Chain Gang: The group of officials on the sidelines that carries the first-down chains and the orange pillars. Two individuals will hold the ends of the chains, starting where the ball is initially placed, to measure ten yards up field. This distance represents the spot where the offense earns a first down.

Downs: The offense gets four downs, or play attempts, to move the ball ten yards toward the end zone before it has to give the ball over to the other team. If they are short of the 10-yard mark after the 4th down, the defense gets the ball at the spot. For example, "2nd and 4" means that this is the team's second down (try) and they have four yards left to gain. For this reason, teams will typically punt on fourth down so that the other team is farther from its end zone when it gets the ball.

Think of this as similar to trying on outfits. Belles can usually stand to try on about three to four outfits. If by the third outfit you don't have a winner, you "punt" and throw on a safe jeans and t-shirt!

Extra Point:

If you are walking into a room of intense fans watching the game, or if you are trying to demonstrate your interest in the game, ask, "What down is it?" You'll actually get a response, and you'll let everyone know you care.

Extra Point: These are not the Gridiron Belle Extra Points you've been reading throughout this book. An extra point during a football game can be earned by kicking the ball through the uprights after a touchdown. An extra point is identical to a field goal in execution, but if it's kicked directly after a touchdown, it is worth only one point (versus a field goal's three points). Similarly, the Gridiron Belles' extra points you'll find in this book will give you that little something extra to get you ahead in the game.

Gridiron: Gridiron is a term commonly used to describe the grid of a football field. We are called Gridiron Belles because we all now understand and appreciate the game of football!

"Half the distance to the goal": The easiest way to describe this phrase is by an example. If the offense is on the 10-yard line getting ready to score and the defense is flagged for a 10-yard holding penalty, then the offense will get the ball on the 5-yard line. Giving the offense the full 10 yards would give them a touchdown, so instead they are given 5 yards—half the distance to the goal.

I-Formation: An offensive formation where the quarterback, full back, and running back line up in a straight line behind the center/ball.

Line of Scrimmage (LOS): Line where the ball is placed at the beginning of each play. The LOS extends from one sideline to the other. Both teams line up on opposing sides of the LOS to start each play. This is also called the neutral zone.

Offensive Plays:

Flea Flicker: Like a flea popping around on your chocolate lab, players in a flea flicker play bounce around so you don't know where to catch them. The quarterback hands the ball off to the running back, making the defense think a running play is underway. Before the running back is tackled, he turns around and pitches the ball back to the quarterback, who then throws the ball downfield. This play basically shifts the entire defense toward the running back, leaving the quarterback wide open.

Lateral: A backward or sideways pass to another player that does not move the ball toward the end zone. There may be only one forward-motion pass in a play, so the running back's pass in a Flea Flicker must be a lateral pass.

Play action: Play Action is one of the most common plays in football. It is intended to slow down the defensive rush. It works like this: The quarterback pretends to hand off the ball to the running back, but he actually keeps it to make a passing play. The quarterback must trick the defense so they'll follow the running back, not the quarterback. It's a must-know for your Belle repertoire.

Shotgun Plays: This has nothing to do with your daddy's firearm. When you hear announcers say that the teams are lined up in "shotgun formation," the quarterback is not getting a handoff directly from the center. Instead, the quarterback is catching a pass from the center. The quarterback will then make the play from the "pocket" (the area about 5-10 yards behind the center, off the line of scrimmage). The idea is to give the quarterback a better view of his open opponents and more time to decide where to throw the ball.

The Option: Teams that run the option are more common than bourbon at a SEC tailgate. The option is a type of running play where the quarterback has *the option* of pitching the ball to a running back behind him or of running the ball himself. With two running backs, there is almost *always* an option.

Wildcat: An offensive formation (made popular in 2006 by Arkansas University, and now used throughout all levels of football: High School, NCAA, NFL). A running back (usually) lines up in the quarterback position and receives the snap (the pass from the center). Primarily a running formation, it relies on misdirection to shock defense and fans.

Zone Read*: The zone read is a running play. The offensive line is in a zone-blocking scheme, which means that instead of blocking one specific player, the line will move in one direction (right or left) and block the first defensive player they see. The quarterback will read one designated defensive player and will have two options, depending on the reaction of the defender. He can either hand the ball to the running back or keep the ball and run himself. He *reads* the defense and acts accordingly. Yes, football players can read (defenses, that are).

Zone Read is extra-point material. If you understand this one, you've nearly mastered football. You might even qualify for calls from offensive coordinators late in the game.

Officials: Seven officials are on the field during the game (technically, not all of the men in stripes are actual referees). Each official has a specific purview, as denoted by the letters on the back of his uniform.

Extra Point:

It's perfectly acceptable for Belles to call all officials referees!

Referee (R): The referee (also known as the Head Referee) wears a white hat rather than the black hats worn by other officials. He usually stands behind the offense on the LOS and is responsible for the details of handoffs (when a player hands the ball to another player). Refs are also responsible for regulating passes, the coin toss at the beginning of the game, and supervising all officials and plays on the field. Referees explain all rulings.

Umpire (U): Don't be confused; you're still strongly discouraged from using the word "inning" during a football game. The Umpire stands behind the defense on the LOS and watches linemen for any sign of illegal blocks or holding.

Head Linesman (HL): You could say that this guy watches the lines. This official stands on the sideline in between the LOS opposite the press box. The Head Linesman is looking for offsides, holding, illegal blocks, or a player stepping out of bounds. The Head Linesman is also responsible for accurate placement of the chain gang and down marker.

Line Judge (LJ): The Line Judge assists the Head Linesman at the opposite end of the LOS and has similar responsibilities. In addition, the Line Judge also determines if a pass was a forward or a lateral pass, and if the ball is passed, punted, or kicked behind the LOS.

● **Field Judge (F or FJ):** This official stands on the same side as the Line Judge and is responsible for counting defensive players. Field Judges also monitor receivers and defenders for pass interference. Basically, he manages all the rules that can be broken in the defensive backfield.

● **Side Judge (S or SJ):** The Side Judge covers his side of the defensive secondary (way back in the defensive back field) on the same side as the Head Linesman. He also keeps an eye on defensive backs and receivers, and he watches closely for pass interference, illegal blocks, or incomplete passes. He is usually responsible for the game and play clock.

● **Back Judge (B or BJ):** Stands deep behind the defensive secondary (the area of field behind the players on the LOS) in the middle (yes, in the middle) of the field. The Back Judge is one of the final judges on whether or not a kick was legal through the uprights.

Offsides: If a defensive player is on the wrong side of the LOS while the ball is snapped, he is offsides, even if he does not touch another player before the ball is snapped.

Extra Point:

If an offensive player moves first, effectively causing the defensive player to move across the LOS, a false-start penalty is called on the offense. This can happen pretty quickly in some instances. That's why commentators will say the defense was pulled offsides (by the offense).

Onside Kick: When a special teams unit during kickoff intentionally kicks the ball short and on the ground. This strategy often allows the kicking team to get to the ball before the other team. The ball, however, must go forward at least ten yards unless the receiving team touches it first. It's like giving a work rival a big job in hopes that she'll mess it up and hand it back over to you.

Over Time: You will often hear over time referred to as OT. Over time is the additional play time that is added to the game if two teams are tied at the end of regulation.

Pass Interference: A penalty in which a defensive player interferes with an offensive player's opportunity to catch the ball while the ball is still in the air. This becomes obvious when a player grabs another player's jersey or arm. If the pass is deemed uncatchable, no penalty is called.

Pick-6: A "pick-6" is the term used to describe an interception returned for a touchdown. The ball is "picked off" or intercepted, and six points are awarded for the touchdown. This terminology is not crucial, but it's certainly good to know for conversations and for understanding commentators.

Pocket: The pocket is easily described as the area protected by the offensive linemen where the quarterback stands after he takes the snap. A slightly more technical way to describe the pocket is "tackle-to-tackle." Imagine drawing two straight lines coming off of the cute backsides of the offensive tackles. The space in between is technically the pocket.

Quarterback Hurry: Hurries are exactly what they sound like. If the defense causes the quarterback to hurry a throw or improvise a play before he wants to, it is a "Quarterback Hurry."

"Red Shirt Ref": When TV stations play commercials during timeouts, the "red shirt ref" stands on the field to delay the game until the network is ready to go live again. When he walks off the field, the TV timeout is finished, and play resumes. Note: You can keep your seat and rest your feet until he walks off the field.

Red-Shirt Freshman: In college sports, the NCAA allows individuals to "red-shirt" one year while they are enrolled in school. During a red-shirt year, the player will participate in all practices and meetings, but he is not allowed to play in a game. This allows players to develop their skills and become familiar with the program. It also gives them an extra year of eligibility. Think of it as an apprenticeship.

Red Zone: The red zone is the last twenty yards of the field before the end zone. Being successful in the Red Zone is said to be vital to a team's success. If a team cannot score within the Red, the offense is considered weak. Conversely, a team needs to have a strong defense within the Red to keep the opponent from scoring.

Rushing Defense: This term refers to the average amount of rushing (running) yards a defense allows its opponents to gain in a game. The lower this number is, the better the defense.

Sack: This is not the brand of purse you had in sixth grade. Sack is a term used to describe tackling the quarterback when he is still holding the ball. While this does not sound very ladylike, in conversations about stats or plays, sacks are music to everyone's ear.

Safety: Two points are awarded when the defense tackles the offense in its own end zone or when the offense commits a penalty in the end zone.

Secondary: The secondary is the defensive area of the field off the line of scrimmage (LOS). The secondary area of the field is where the two cornerbacks and two safeties start the play. The secondary focuses on defending against wide receivers (WR) and a quarterback (QB) or running back (RB) who breaks through the defensive line.

Skill Player: Skill players are players who handle the football (i.e., quarterbacks, running backs, receivers, punters, place kickers). Basically, more skill is necessary for these positions than for players whose primary job is plowing into an opponent.

Slot Receiver: A wide receiver who starts closer to the ball than the other wide receivers. A slot receiver must start in the back field (off the line). He's a sneaky little guy. Well, actually he's tall but deceiving at the start of the play.

Spread Offense: A spread offense is as common as monogrammed towels for a graduation present. This offense uses more wide receivers (WR) than running backs (RB) and spreads them across the whole field, in an attempt to spread out a defense. Offenses that run "the spread" generally throw the ball more often.

Special Teams: A special teams unit is present during a punt, punt return, kickoff, kickoff return, and field goal. As a general rule, any time the ball is being kicked, the special teams unit is on the field.

Spot Foul: A term used to describe a penalty where the ball is placed at the spot where the foul takes place versus specific yardage from the LOS.

Taking a Knee: Sorry, Belles, we're not talking about him popping the big question here. A quarterback will "take a knee" to waste time. The quarterback will receive the snap (the pass from the center) and immediately go to his knee, "downing the ball" inbounds. Thus, the clock continues to run, but the offense loses a down. The clock keeps running, but the offense keeps the defense from rushing.

Three and Out: The term "Three and Out" refers to an offense's attempt to gain a first down. When an offense runs three plays and is not able to gain a first down, they will normally punt on fourth down. Three plays, and you're out! The ball is awarded to the other team.

Three-Step-Drop: The quarterback receives the ball from the center, takes three quick steps back, and makes a speedy pass to an open receiver. Belles generally take a three-step-drop when it's necessary to create distance between aggressive suitors before quickly deciding which Gent is to accompany her to Saturday's game.

Touchback: The result of a play where the ball is deemed dead after it crosses a team's own goal line. A touchback often occurs because of a fumble, interception (if intercepted while in the end zone), a long punt, or a kickoff. The ball is then placed on the 20-yard line to begin the next play.

Touchdown: A touchdown occurs when the ball is either carried into, fumbled into or caught, in the end zone. A touchdown earns the team six points and you a kiss from your date! Referees hold both arms straight in the air to signal a touchdown. Feel free to throw yours up too, showcasing your touchdown purse!

True Freshmen: True freshmen are players in their first year of school, who do not take a red shirt year. They are eligible to play in all games, but they have only four years of eligibility to play in the NCAA. True freshmen are generally really good, hence they do not wait a year to play once on the team!

Special Thanks:

I wrote this book in honor of my grandmothers, the spirited women who taught me to recognize "pass interference" (and not to be afraid to yell at the ref who missed the call), the importance of seven men on the line, and how to appreciate the attractive qualities of quarterbacks. I wrote this book for my girlfriends, namely my sister, all of whom have been missing out on the glory that is college football. I wrote this book because football, while played by men, is made truly enjoyable by us, the Gridiron Belles. The tradition of civility on Saturdays in the South is, in its purest form, a tradition that must be passed to the next generation.

A special thanks to: All of my game day hosts along the way, Colleen Clemons (Auburn '04); the Dyer and Richardson Families and gang (Ole Miss '06); Calhoun Hipp, III (South Carolina '07); Mark Robinson (Georgia '07); the Massey family (Florida v Georgia '08); Carey Roussel; Lauren, Vivian and John Bordelon (LSU '09); Susannah and Adam de'Nobriga (Mississippi State '10); Molly Smith and Nate Hulling (Tennessee '10); Susan "Ken" Truss (Alabama '10); Sarah Hart (Florida '10); Bart Shelley (Arkansas '10); Grace and Curt Johnson (Vanderbilt '10); Pat Manning (Auburn '10); Craig Mueller and Michele Stokan (SEC Championship '10).

All of the Gents in my life, especially my grandfather, Ken Porco, who helped me understand the game of football. Thank you for letting me watch the games with the guys and letting me think I was part of the team (Rhodes College SAEs and football Lynx Cats). Thank you, Calhoun, for your patience while I asked countless questions. Thank you, Matthew, for poking fun at me for the many teams and quarterbacks I have given my heart to through the years and sharing genuine ideas about a pink airstream. Thank you for answering texts, e-mails and countless phone calls when I needed clarification, Bart Law, Pat, Z, Calhoun, "Jack," Pop, and Lambert. Thank you all for your never-ending support and encouragement throughout this endeavor. Thank you Mr. Brian Jones, for serving as my much needed attorney.

To Lauren Roussel Bordelon for teaching me about SEC traditions, pride, and colors (LSU is *gold*, not yellow). Thank you for being my biggest fan and for vowing to raise our daughters and sons to be ladies and gentlemen with double names. Thank you for the countless books, articles, and ideas we have shared on becoming the best Southerners we can be.

To T.J. "Jack" Massey for being the most spirited and dedicated football fan I've ever known–thank you for teaching me the true meaning of team loyalty and loving me despite my allegiance to Auburn. Thank you from the bottom of my heart for always encouraging me to finish the book and co-dreaming with me of box seats at both Auburn and Florida. I am beyond thankful for you sharing your Gators, family traditions, and Betty & R.L. with me. I am forever grateful for the Massey family's generosity of tickets, recipes, and Gator talk. "If you aren't a Gator, you must be Gator bait."

Bart Law Shelley, my favorite quaterback, for inviting me to the best Arkansas game ever played in Fayetteville and for also going with me to one of the worst. Thank you for the countless hours of conversations about recruits, coaches, wins and losses, pre-season picks, Big 12 versus SEC football, and for clarifying my vocab definitions. I hope you become an SEC coach one day.

Lizzie Ferreri Petticrew, my-editor-in-chief, thank you for the countless corrections, reminders, and red lines on my work. Somehow I appreciate you asking the questions I didn't want to answer and making the suggestions I didn't want to hear. Thank you for the hours you spent becoming nauseous over the obsession of SEC football—*you* made it work. I am eternally grateful.

My daddy, for challenging me to be the best Southern tailgate writer I could be. Thank you for encouraging me to capitalize on my passion for football and etiquette and to always think outside the box but never outside the SEC. Thank you for your "top 5 ideas" and for coaching me throughout the years on how to be a *Champ*... I'll be loving you always.

My Sweet Mama, for generously testing nearly every recipe I gathered while touring the South and not being upset when I decided not to use a single one for this book! Thank you for keeping the late games on, even when you were "just resting your eyes;" thank you for introducing me to pearls, teaching me how to be a hostess and, above all, a Southern lady.

My beautiful sister, who despises football and questions the sanity of all football fans. Thank you for being my wing-Belle, for strongly influencing my game day apparel, and for coining the term, "touchdown purse." Thank you for enduring the agony I caused you by asking you to actually read this book. Without your loathing of whistles, this book may never have gone to print.

I appreciate everyone who listened to me whistle Dixie about *Gridiron Belles* until I got serious. A special thanks to all of my editors along the way: Adrienne Sobolak, Macy McBeth, Pam Richardson, Natalia Sylvester, Greer Wymond, Christina Martell, Scott Stortz and Carol Butler. Thank you to everyone who called an SEC friend on my behalf, invited me to a tailgate, gave me tickets, answered a questionnaire, sent in pictures, signed a consent form, told me an SEC story, or listened to me when I wanted to talk about football and pearls. An entire SEC village was necessary to pull this book together. If I haven't already sent you a handwritten thank-you note, I owe you one!

Bibliography

Alabama:

Songs of Alabama:

http://www.rolltide.com/trads/song-downloads.html

National Championships:

http://www.rolltide.com/trads/national-championships.html

Arkansas:

Arkansas Athletics:

http://www.arkansasrazorbacks.com/ViewArticle.dbml?DB_OEM_ID=6100&ATCLID=294564

Auburn:

Auburn Football:

http://auburntigers.cstv.com/trads/aub-trads.html

Florida:

Traditions:

http://www.gatorzone.com/multimedia/?p=traditions

History:

http://www.gatorzone.com/football/history.php

Georgia:

Georgia Traditions

http://www.georgiadogs.com/ot/geo-traditions.html

Georgia Championships:

http://www.georgiadogs.com/ot/geo-championships.html

Kentucky:

Traditions and Songs:

http://www.ukathletics.com/trads/songs.html

History and Archives

http://www.ukathletics.com/sports/m-footbl/archive/kty-m-footbl-archive.html

LSU:

LSU Championship Seasons

http://www.lsusports.net/ViewArticle.dbml?SPSID=27815&SPID=2164&DB_LANG=C&DB_OEM_ID=5200&ATCLID=177163

LSU Football

http://www.lsusports.net/ViewArticle.dbml?DB_OEM_ID=5200&ATCLID=177310

Mississippi State:

Ms State Traditions:

http://www.mstateathletics.com/ViewArticle.dbml?DB_OEM_ID=16800&ATCLID=926236

Ole Miss:

History of Rebel Football:

http://www.olemisssports.com/sports/m-footbl/spec-rel/rebels-football-history.html

South Carolina:

Gamecock Traditions:

http://gamecocksonline.cstv.com/trads/scar-trads.html

Tennessee:

Tennessee Traditions:

http://www.utsports.com/fans/traditions.html

Tennessee SEC Championships:

http://www.utsports.com/fans/sec.html

Tennessee NCAA Championships

http://www.utsports.com/fans/ncaa.html

Vanderbilt:

Vanderbilt Spirit and Songs

http://www.vanderbilt.edu/spirit/songs.html

Vanderbilt Band:

http://www.vanderbilt.edu/vuband/

SEC Heisman Trophy Winners:
http://www.heisman.com/winners/hsmn-winners.html

SEC teams and championships:
http://www.secdigitalnetwork.com/SECSPORTS/SPORTS/2010FootballChampionship.aspx